Master React in 5 Days

Become a React Expert in Under a Week

Eric Sarrion

Apress®

Master React in 5 Days: Become a React Expert in Under a Week

Eric Sarrion
VIRY CHATILLON, France

ISBN-13 (pbk): 978-1-4842-9854-1   ISBN-13 (electronic): 978-1-4842-9855-8
https://doi.org/10.1007/978-1-4842-9855-8

Managing Director, Apress Media LLC: Welmoed Spahr
Acquisitions Editor: Divya Modi
Development Editor: James Markham

Cover designed by eStudioCalamar
Cover image designed by Freepik (www.freepik.com)

Distributed to the book trade worldwide by Springer Science+Business Media New York, 1 New York Plaza, Suite 4600, New York, NY 10004-1562, USA. Phone 1-800-SPRINGER, fax (201) 348-4505, e-mail orders-ny@springer-sbm.com, or visit www.springeronline.com. Apress Media, LLC is a California LLC and the sole member (owner) is Springer Science + Business Media Finance Inc (SSBM Finance Inc). SSBM Finance Inc is a **Delaware** corporation.

For information on translations, please e-mail booktranslations@springernature.com; for reprint, paperback, or audio rights, please e-mail bookpermissions@springernature.com.

Apress titles may be purchased in bulk for academic, corporate, or promotional use. eBook versions and licenses are also available for most titles. For more information, reference our Print and eBook Bulk Sales web page at http://www.apress.com/bulk-sales.

Any source code or other supplementary material referenced by the author in this book is available to readers on GitHub (https://github.com/Apress/Master-React-in-5-Days-by-Eric-Sarrion). For more detailed information, please visit https://www.apress.com/gp/services/source-code.

Paper in this product is recyclable.

Table of Contents

About the Author

Eric Sarrion is a trainer, web developer, and an independent consultant. He has been involved in all kinds of IT projects for over 30 years. He is also a longtime author of web development technologies and is renowned for the clarity of his explanations and examples. He resides in Paris, France.

About the Technical Reviewer

Kenneth Fukizi is a software engineer, architect, and consultant with experience in coding on different platforms internationally. Prior to dedicated software development, he worked as a lecturer and was then head of IT at different organizations. He has domain experience working with technology for companies mainly in the financial sector. When he's not working, he likes reading up on emerging technologies and strives to be an active member of the software community. Kenneth currently leads a community of African developers, through a startup company called AfrikanCoder.

Acknowledgments

I would like to thank Gabriel Bieules (Austin, Texas), a specialist in React development, for his valuable reviews and contributions to the book.

Introduction

Discover how to master React in record time with the book *Master React in 5 Days*. Are you dreaming of learning this revolutionary technology without spending months on endless tutorials? This book is tailor-made for you! In just five days, you will acquire the fundamental skills to develop exceptional React applications.

Dive into an accelerated learning method that will propel your progress by leaps and bounds. Each chapter is carefully designed to teach you the essential concepts of React, such as components, props, state, events, life cycle, and hooks, without wasting time on complex explanations.

Thanks to clear and accessible language, you will be immersed in the intricacies of React from the very first page. Code examples are accompanied by detailed explanations, allowing you to quickly grasp the nuances of this technology. You don't need to be a programming expert; the book is suitable for all levels, from beginners to more experienced developers looking to acquaint themselves with React.

Each chapter includes practical exercises to immediately apply what you learn. You'll have the opportunity to create your own React applications, thereby enhancing your understanding and solidifying your skills. You'll be amazed at how rapidly you progress with this hands-on approach.

Master React in 5 Days is much more than just a book; it's a comprehensive resource that guides you step by step on your learning journey. Whether you prefer to follow the book independently or use it in conjunction with other online resources, it will provide you with a strong foundation to unleash the full potential of React.

So, are you ready to take on the challenge and become a proficient React developer in just five days? Don't wait any longer! Dive into this exciting adventure right now. The book *Master React in 5 Days* will open the doors to a world of endless possibilities in web development.

CHAPTER 1

Day 1: Mastering Component Writing with React

This chapter serves as our starting point for learning how to create components using the JavaScript library React.

React is an open source library used to create interactive user interfaces for web applications. By using React, you can build reusable components to construct rich and scalable user interfaces.

In this chapter, you will learn the basics of creating React components and build your first component. We will also review the fundamental principles of JSX, a syntax used to create React elements, and how to integrate it into our code.

You will develop a solid understanding of React's foundational principles by creating simple components, ready to be integrated into larger projects. This hands-on approach will allow you to absorb the essential basics of React while preparing you to collaborate on more extensive projects.

Ready to get started? Let's go!

© Eric Sarrion 2023

E. Sarrion, *Master React in 5 Days*, https://doi.org/10.1007/978-1-4842-9855-8_1

Why Use React

React is an open source JavaScript library created by Facebook for building complex user interfaces. It has gained popularity due to its ease of use and flexibility in creating modern web applications.

Here are a few reasons why React is user-friendly and popular:

1. Reusable components: React is built on the concept of components, which are reusable blocks of code that can be combined to construct a complex user interface. This approach saves time by allowing developers to build applications from modular building blocks.

2. Virtual DOM: React employs a technique called the Virtual DOM to enhance user interface performance. The Virtual DOM is an in-memory representation of the user interface's state. When a user interacts with the application's user interface, React compares the current state of the Virtual DOM with the previous representation and updates the view (i.e., what is displayed) only for elements that have changed. This approach is faster than traditional methods of updating the user interface, making React more efficient and performant.

3. Large community and documentation: React is backed by a large community of developers who regularly contribute to the library. This means there are plenty of resources available for learning React, including comprehensive documentation,

quick start guides, code examples, and educational videos. This abundance of resources makes learning React easier for new developers, and this book is a part of it.

4. Multi-platform support: React can be used to develop web, mobile, and desktop applications. It's also possible to integrate React with other libraries and frameworks, making it a versatile choice for multi-platform application development.

5. React Native: React Native is a framework that allows developers to build native mobile applications using React syntax. This approach enables developers to create mobile apps from the same source code used for web applications. This approach reduces costs and accelerates mobile app development.

6. Comprehensive ecosystem: React integrates well with a wide range of tools and libraries for application development, such as Redux, GraphQL, Next.js, Gatsby, Material UI, etc. This integration makes it easier to create quality applications with advanced features and superior performance.

In conclusion, React's ease of use and popularity stem from its modularity, Virtual DOM approach, large developer community, and versatility for multi-platform application development. The ability to create reusable components, along with integration with React Native and a comprehensive ecosystem of tools and libraries, makes it an ideal choice for developers looking to create modern and scalable web applications.

React Virtual DOM

In React, the Virtual DOM (Document Object Model) is an in-memory representation of the actual DOM (the HTML representation of elements displayed on the page). When changes are made to a React component, instead of directly updating the actual DOM, React first updates the Virtual DOM, which is a virtual representation of the real DOM. Of course, updating the Virtual DOM is much faster than updating the actual DOM, which is why using it is beneficial.

After updating the Virtual DOM, React performs a process called "reconciliation," where it compares the new Virtual DOM with the previous version of the Virtual DOM. This process determines the minimal number of changes that need to be made to the actual DOM to reflect the component's modifications (see example in the next section).

This approach offers several advantages. Firstly, it allows React to optimize the process of updating the actual DOM, resulting in faster and more efficient updates. Additionally, it enables developers to write their components independently of the browser and underlying DOM, making it easier to create complex user interfaces that are consistent across different browsers and devices.

Step 1: Creating the Virtual DOM

React creates a virtual tree using components defined in JavaScript code. Each component describes how a part of the user interface should be displayed based on the application's state. When the state changes, React regenerates the virtual tree by traversing the components and updating their virtual representations. This step serves as preparation for reconciliation, where React compares the newly created virtual tree with the old one to determine the changes.

Step 2: Reconciliation Process

Reconciliation in React is the process by which React compares the virtual tree representing the current state of the user interface with a previous version to determine which parts of the user interface need to be updated. The goal of reconciliation is to optimize performance by avoiding re-rendering the entire element tree with each update.

Here's a simple example of reconciliation in React:

Let's assume we have a React component called App that displays a counter and a button to increment the counter by 1 on each click.

The code in the example that follows will be explained in the next sections. The key point here is to understand how the reconciliation process works.

File: App.js

```
import React, { useState } from 'react';

function App() {
  const [count, setCount] = useState(0);

  const handleIncrement = () => {
    setCount(count + 1);
  };

  return (
    <div>
      <h2>Counter: {count}</h2>
      <button onClick={handleIncrement}>Increment</button>
    </div>
  );
};

export default App;
```

Now, let's assume the user clicks the Increment button multiple times. With each click, React updates the counter's state and triggers a reconciliation process to update the user interface.

Here's what happens during reconciliation:

1. The user clicks the button, triggering the handleIncrement() function.

2. The handleIncrement() function updates the counter's state with the new value.

3. React compares the virtual tree representing the current state of the user interface with the previous version.

4. React determines which parts of the user interface have changed by comparing the differences between the virtual trees. It recognizes that the value 0 has become 1, following the first click on the Increment button.

5. React updates only the parts that have changed in the actual DOM, rather than re-rendering the entire element tree.

For example, let's say the counter has been incremented by 1, changing from 0 to 1. The virtual tree before and after the update looks like this:

Before the Update

```
<div>
  <h2> Counter: 0</h2>
  <button>Increment</button>
</div>
```

After the Update

```
<div>
  <h2> Counter: 1</h2>
  <button>Increment</button>
</div>
```

In this example, React notices that only the counter value has changed (0 became 1). It will update the relevant part of the DOM to reflect this change without touching other parts of the DOM.

This is how React optimizes performance by using reconciliation to update only the parts of the user interface that have actually changed, minimizing the number of expensive DOM manipulation operations.

Decomposing an Application into Components

Decomposing an application into components, as suggested by React, is a common practice in software development. This allows for creating a modular structure that facilitates code maintenance, reusability, and understanding.

Here's a simple example of decomposing an application into components:

Let's say we want to build an application that displays a list of tasks to do, each with a check box to indicate whether the task is completed or not.

The first step would be to divide the application into two main components: a parent component TaskList and a child component TaskItem.

The parent component TaskList would be responsible for managing the complete list of tasks to do. It would handle retrieving the list data from a data source (e.g., an API or a database), sorting, filtering, and passing them down to the child component TaskItem (see Figure 1-1).

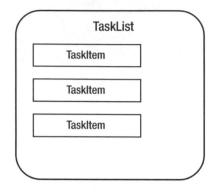

Figure 1-1. *TaskList and TaskItem components*

The child component, TaskItem, on the other hand, would be responsible for displaying an individual task. It would display the task name and a check box to indicate whether the task is completed or not. This component would be reusable and display a task item each time it is called by the parent component, TaskList.

Next, we could further decompose the TaskList component into sub-components, such as TaskListHeader (for the list header), TaskListFooter (for the list footer), or TaskListFilter (for managing filters in the list) (see Figure 1-2).

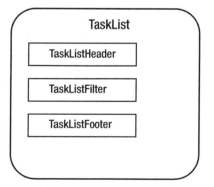

Figure 1-2. *Components TaskList, TaskListHeader, TaskListFilter, and TaskListFooter*

Lastly, we could also decompose the TaskItem component into sub-components, such as TaskName (for displaying the task name), TaskCheckbox (for displaying the check box), or TaskDueDate (for displaying the task due date) (see Figure 1-3).

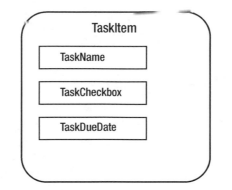

Figure 1-3. *Components TaskItem, TaskName, TaskCheckbox, and TaskDueDate*

By decomposing our application into components, we have created a modular structure that facilitates code understanding, maintenance, and reusability. Additionally, since each component is responsible for a specific task, it makes debugging easier, as each part can be managed individually.

Creating a First React Application

The simplest way to use React in our applications is to use the create-react-app command, which sets up the minimal architecture of a functional React application.

The create-react-app command becomes available after installing the create-react-app module using the npm command. The npm command is accessible after installing Node.js. Install Node.js if it's not already installed.

Once the prerequisites are in place, you can enter the "npm install -g create-react-app" command in a command prompt to install the create-react-app module (see Figure 1-4).

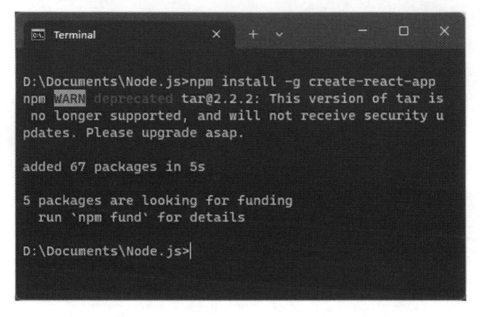

Figure 1-4. *Installation of the create-react-app module*

Once the module is installed, the create-react-app command is accessible to enable the creation of our React applications.

Let's then enter the command "create-react-app reactapp". This command creates the "reactapp" application that will work using React.

After entering this command, the application begins to be created. The application creation process takes some time as the modules required for the application's functioning are downloaded from the Internet (see Figure 1-5).

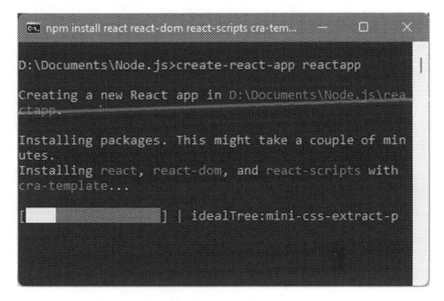

Figure 1-5. *React application being created*

Then, at the end of the creation of the reactapp application, you will get the screen shown in Figure 1-6.

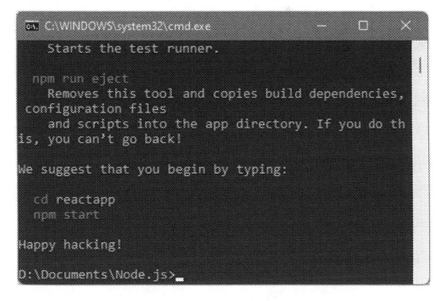

Figure 1-6. *Completion of React application creation*

Once the application is created, simply enter the suggested commands in the command prompt: these commands are "cd reactapp", followed by "npm start".

The "npm start" command starts an HTTP server based on Node.js, which will allow you to view your React application in a web browser. The server that's started listens for connections on port 3000, as indicated in the command prompt window in Figure 1-7.

```
Windows PowerShell                           —    □    ×

D:\Documents\Node.js>cd reactapp

D:\Documents\Node.js\reactapp>npm start

> reactapp@0.1.0 start
> react-scripts start

(node:8932) [DEP_WEBPACK_DEV_SERVER_ON_AFTER_SETUP_MI
DDLEWARE] DeprecationWarning: 'onAfterSetupMiddleware
' option is deprecated. Please use the 'setupMiddlewa
res' option.
(Use `node --trace-deprecation ...` to show where the
 warning was created)
(node:8932) [DEP_WEBPACK_DEV_SERVER_ON_BEFORE_SETUP_M
IDDLEWARE] DeprecationWarning: 'onBeforeSetupMiddlewa
re' option is deprecated. Please use the 'setupMiddle
wares' option.
Starting the development server...
Compiled successfully!

You can now view reactapp in the browser.

  Local:            http://localhost:3000
  On Your Network:  http://192.168.1.26:3000

Note that the development build is not optimized.
To create a production build, use npm run build.

webpack compiled successfully
```

Figure 1-7. *Starting the server containing the React application*

Now, let's establish a connection with the server by using the URL
http://localhost:3000 as shown in the window in Figure 1-8. Type this URL
into your web browser.

13

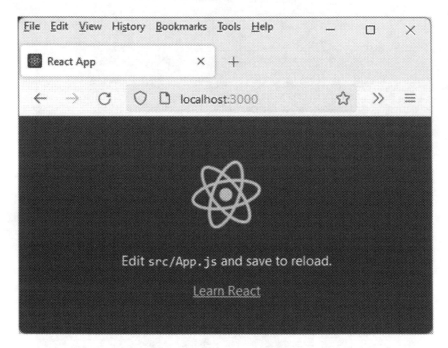

Figure 1-8. *Display of the URL http://localhost:3000*

In the web browser, you will see the "reactapp" application that we created using the "create-react-app" command.

The "reactapp" application is built with React and is located in the "reactapp" directory. Now, let's explore the files and directories within the application directory.

Analyzing the Main Files of the React Application

The previously displayed page corresponds to the index.html page located in the public directory of the application (with the application itself situated in the reactapp directory).

The other main files of the React application are located in the src directory of the application. In this directory, you will mainly find the index.js and App.js files:

- The index.js file is the one loaded first when displaying the index.html page.

- The App.js file represents the App component of the application, which serves as the global component. This file is loaded from the index.js file.

In the following sections, you'll find the contents of these two files, starting with the index.js file.

Step 1: Contents of the index.js File

Let's explore the contents of the index.js file located in the src directory of the application.

File: src/index.js

```
import React from 'react';
import ReactDOM from 'react-dom/client';
import './index.css';
import App from './App';
import reportWebVitals from './reportWebVitals';

const root = ReactDOM.createRoot(document.
getElementById('root'));
root.render(
  <React.StrictMode>
    <App />
  </React.StrictMode>
);
```

15

```
// If you want to start measuring performance in your app, pass
    a function
// to log results (for example: reportWebVitals(console.log))
// or send to an analytics endpoint. Learn more: https://bit.ly/
    CRA-vitals
reportWebVitals();
```

Let's describe the code written in the previous index.js file. We start by importing the core React modules, namely, React and ReactDOM, into the index.js file using JavaScript's import statements.

The import statement in JavaScript is used to import one or more functionalities from a directory or file where they are defined. Once these functionalities are imported, they become accessible within the module that imports them.

The React and ReactDOM modules are located in the node_modules directory, which is automatically created when the "reactapp" application is generated using the create-react-app command:

- The React module contains the code of the React library.

- The ReactDOM module is specialized for using React in HTML pages (React can also be used in native mobile applications under the name React Native).

Next, we import the App component from the App.js file using the import statement: "import App from './App'". We can see the usage of the App component in the parameter of the root.render() method. The root.render() method is used to indicate the HTML code that will be inserted into the HTML element with the id "root".

The App component is written here in the form <App />, which is the syntax used for writing components with React. This writing style is called JSX and is similar to XML. Notice that we write JSX code without surrounding it with quotes (we write <App /> instead of "<App />"), because what we are writing here is not a string but represents JSX code, which is then transformed into HTML code during the execution of the React program.

The <React.StrictMode> element included in the JSX code of the index. js file allows displaying additional information in the JavaScript console in case of errors. You can find more information at `https://react.dev/reference/react/StrictMode`.

The JavaScript console is typically displayed by pressing the F12 key on the keyboard.

The element with the id "root" is obtained with the instruction root = ReactDOM.createRoot(document.getElementById('root')). If you view the contents of the index.html file located in the public directory, you will see that the only HTML code in the index.html page corresponds to a <div> element with the id "root" (written as <div id="root"></div>). It is within this <div> element that the HTML code created during the root.render() method call will be inserted.

Let's take a look at the contents of the index.html file.

Step 2: Contents of the index.html File

Here is the content of the index.html file in the public directory of the application, where we have highlighted the <div> element:

File: public/index.html

```
<!DOCTYPE html>
<html lang="en">
  <head>
    <meta charset="utf-8" />
    <link rel="icon" href="%PUBLIC_URL%/favicon.ico" />
    <meta name="viewport" content="width=device-width,
    initial-scale=1" />
```

```html
    <meta name="theme-color" content="#000000" />
    <meta
      name="description"
      content="Web site created using create-react-app"
    />
    <link rel="apple-touch-icon" href="%PUBLIC_URL%/
    logo192.png" />
    <!--
      manifest.json provides metadata used when your web app
      is installed on a user's mobile device or desktop. See
      https://developers.google.com/web/fundamentals/web-app-
      manifest/
    -->
    <link rel="manifest" href="%PUBLIC_URL%/manifest.json" />
    <!--
      Notice the use of %PUBLIC_URL% in the tags above.
      It will be replaced with the URL of the `public` folder
      during the build.
      Only files inside the `public` folder can be referenced
      from the HTML.

      Unlike "/favicon.ico" or "favicon.ico", "%PUBLIC_URL%/
      favicon.ico" will work correctly both with client-side
      routing and a non-root public URL.
      Learn how to configure a non-root public URL by running
      `npm run build`.
    -->
    <title>React App</title>
  </head>
  <body>
```

```
<noscript>You need to enable JavaScript to run this app.</
noscript>
<div id="root"></div>
<!--
    This HTML file is a template.
    If you open it directly in the browser, you will see an
    empty page.

    You can add webfonts, meta tags, or analytics to
    this file.
    The build step will place the bundled scripts into the
    <body> tag.

    To begin the development, run `npm start` or
    `yarn start`.
    To create a production bundle, use `npm run build` or
    `yarn build`.
    -->
  </body>
</html>
```

Step 3: Contents of the App.js File

Let's now take a look at the contents of the App.js file, which corresponds to the App component. This component is then used in the form <App /> in JSX (see src/index.js).

App Component (file src/App.js)

```
import logo from './logo.svg';
import './App.css';

function App() {
```

```
  return (
    <div className="App">
      <header className="App-header">
        <img src={logo} className="App-logo" alt="logo" />
        <p>
          Edit <code>src/App.js</code> and save to reload.
        </p>
        <a
          className="App-link"
          href="https://reactjs.org"
          target="_blank"
          rel="noopener noreferrer"
        >
          Learn React
        </a>
      </header>
    </div>
  );
}

export default App;
```

Let's describe the content of the preceding App component. It corresponds to a function App() that returns JSX code. This JSX code will be transformed into HTML code when the App component is rendered. The App() function is then exported at the end of the module, making it accessible for other modules that use it (especially in index.js as seen earlier).

Here, we can see that a React component is a simple JavaScript function that returns the JSX code that will be rendered when the component is displayed.

Now, let's briefly explain what JSX syntax is in React. As it's a very important topic in React, the next chapter will also be entirely dedicated to it.

JSX Syntax in React

JSX code in React is a syntax that allows you to write UI elements by combining JavaScript and HTML in a familiar and expressive way. This makes creating UIs in React simpler and more readable

The term JSX stands for JavaScript and XML. The XML elements used here will either be traditional HTML elements written in XML syntax or React components that we create ourselves.

In JSX, you can write UI elements as if you were writing HTML code, but you can also embed JavaScript code inside these elements. This means you can create custom components, manage application logic and state, and interact with data using JavaScript, all while using a familiar syntax to structure your UI.

Here's an example of JSX in React:

File: App.js

```
import React from "react";
function App() {
  const name = "John Doe";
  const greeting = <h1>Hi, {name} !</h1>;
  return (
    <div>
      {greeting}
      <p>This is an example of JSX code in React..</p>
      <button>Click</button>
    </div>
  );
};
export default App;
```

In this example, we have a functional component App that uses JSX to define the structure of the user interface, corresponding here to the <div> element returned by the function. We also use JavaScript variables (such as "name") to dynamically generate content in our user interface. JavaScript variables used in the JSX code are enclosed in curly braces (like {name}) to indicate that it's a JavaScript statement we want to evaluate.

The JSX code is then converted into plain JavaScript code to be executed in the browser. This means that JSX code is ultimately interpreted as React function calls to create UI elements.

JSX code is widely used in the React ecosystem because it offers a convenient and concise way to create user interfaces while harnessing the power of JavaScript to manage application logic and state.

JSX code consists of traditional HTML elements like shown earlier, but can also involve React components. Now, let's see how to create our own React components by following this pattern.

Creating a First React Component

We want to create a Counter component that displays an incrementing counter automatically every second. The component will be used in the form <Counter />. We'll learn step by step how to create this component.

The App.js file is modified to display the Counter component, used in the form <Counter /> in JSX. The Counter component will be defined in the Counter.js file, located in the same src directory as the App.js file.

Here's the description of the App.js and Counter.js files:

App Component (file src/App.js)

```
import logo from './logo.svg';
import './App.css';
import Counter from "./Counter.js";
```

```
function App() {
  return (
    <Counter />
  );
}

export default App;
```

Counter Component (file src/Counter.js)

```
function Counter() {
  var count = 0;
  return (
    <>
    The counter is set to: {count}
    </>
  )
}

export default Counter;
```

We can make two (important) observations about the Counter component code:

- • We use an empty element without specifying any tag inside it. This element ends with, and it allows us to group one or more HTML elements or React components inside it. The JSX code provided (as the return value of the function) must be well-formed, meaning it should have a root element that encloses the other elements. We could have used <div> as the root element, but that would create an unnecessary

<div> element that doesn't need to be there. The
advantage of using is that this element won't be
inserted into the DOM tree, unlike <div> which would
be inserted if used.

- We use the curly braces {} notation, here to display the
  value of the "count" variable as {count}. React uses this
  notation to write JavaScript expressions in the returned
  JSX code. Here, we indicate {count} to obtain the value
  of the "count" variable, but we could also have used
  {count+10} as count+10 is also a JavaScript expression.

Let's also modify the App.css file, which contains the defined styles in
the application. We replace the existing lines with these:

Application Styles (file src/App.css)

```
body {
  margin:10px;
}
```

A margin of 10px is specified around the HTML page to ensure that
displayed texts are not too close to the edges of the window.

The new page is displayed directly in the browser using the URL http://
localhost:3000. Below the window (by pressing the F12 key), the console
is displayed, allowing you to view texts displayed by console.log() in our
programs, as well as any informational or error messages (see Figure 1-9).

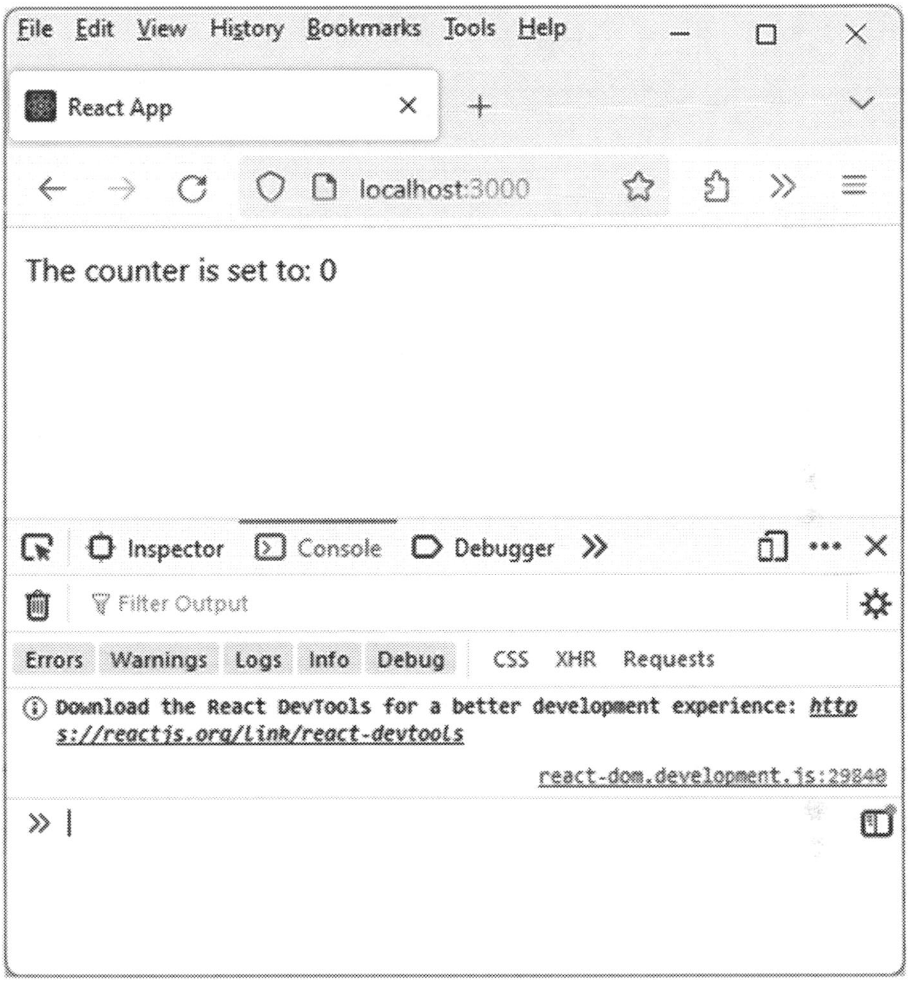

Figure 1-9. *Display of the Counter component*

A helpful tip is displayed in the console, suggesting to download the React DevTools utility, which allows you to visualize React components on the displayed page.

Let's click the link provided in the console and install this utility in the browser being used.

Step 1: Install React DevTools

React employs a set of specific tools, known as React DevTools, that provide assistance in developing React applications.

Once React DevTools is installed (by clicking the previous link displayed in the console), the console window will have two additional tabs (Components and Profiler tabs) (see Figure 1-10).

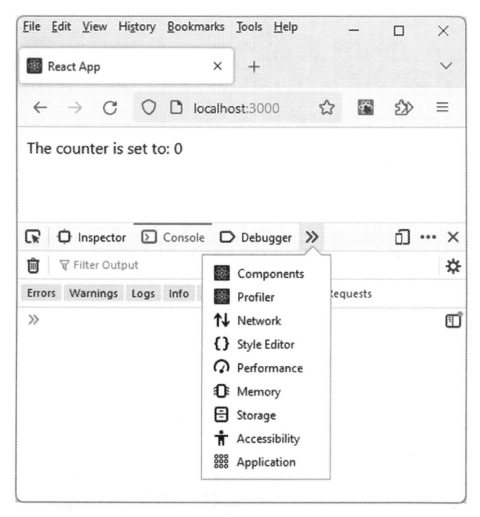

Figure 1-10. *Using React DevTools*

Let's select the Components tab from the list. A description of the React components used in the application will appear. The component hierarchy of App and Counter can be found there. This will be particularly useful during application debugging (see Figure 1-11).

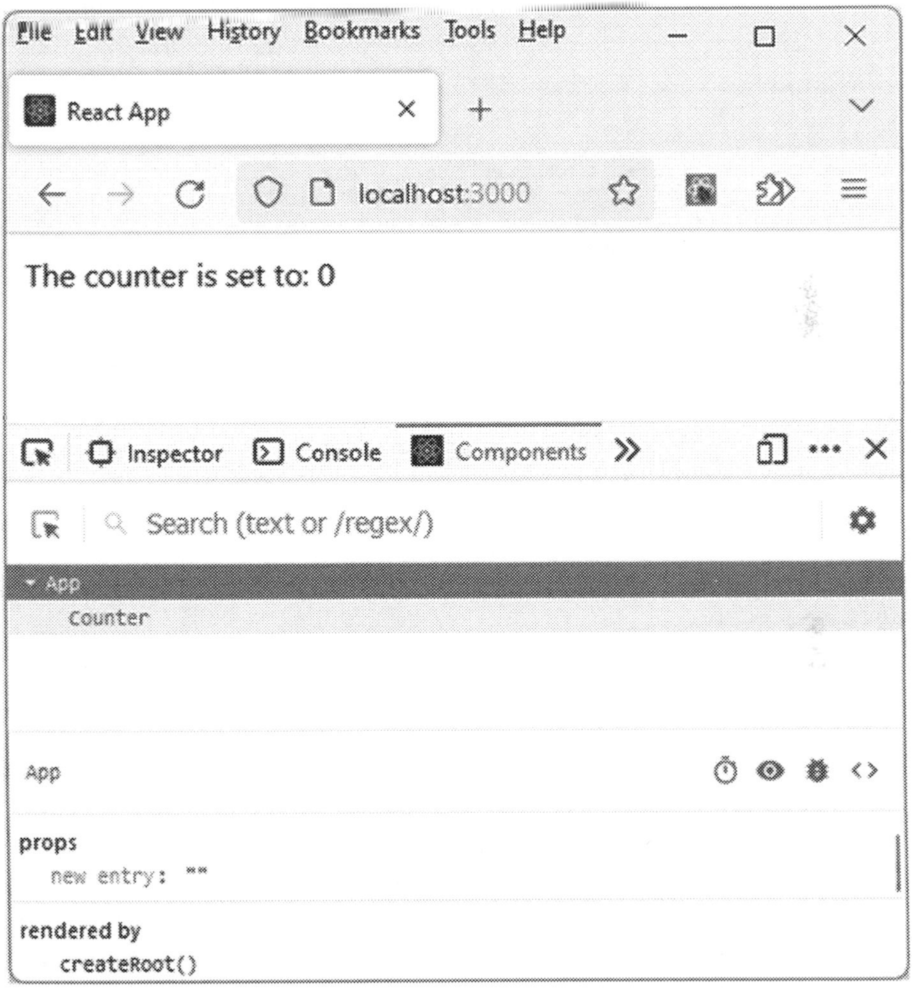

Figure 1-11. *Display of components in React DevTools*

Let's continue writing the program. Now we need to increment the displayed counter, which currently remains at 0. To achieve this, we will use JavaScript's setInterval() function.

In the following example, the code we are going to write may not be exactly what we would write directly if we knew the internal workings of React. However, the gradual approach we are taking will help us understand how React works by discovering it step by step.

Step 2: Incrementing the Counter with setInterval( )

JavaScript's setInterval(callback, timeout) function allows us to trigger a process at regular intervals. The process to be executed is specified in the callback function provided as a parameter to the function. The process will be executed at every timeout milliseconds, unless the clearInterval() function is called to stop the recurring process.

Using setInterval() to increment the counter (file src/Counter.js)

```
function Counter() {
  var count = 0;

  setInterval(function() {
    count++;
    console.log("count =", count);
  }, 1000);

  return (
    <>
    The counter is set to: {count}
    </>
  )
}

export default Counter;
```

Let's run this program in the browser, displaying the console window to view the value of the counter. This counter value is also displayed on the HTML page using the expression {count} (see Figure 1-12).

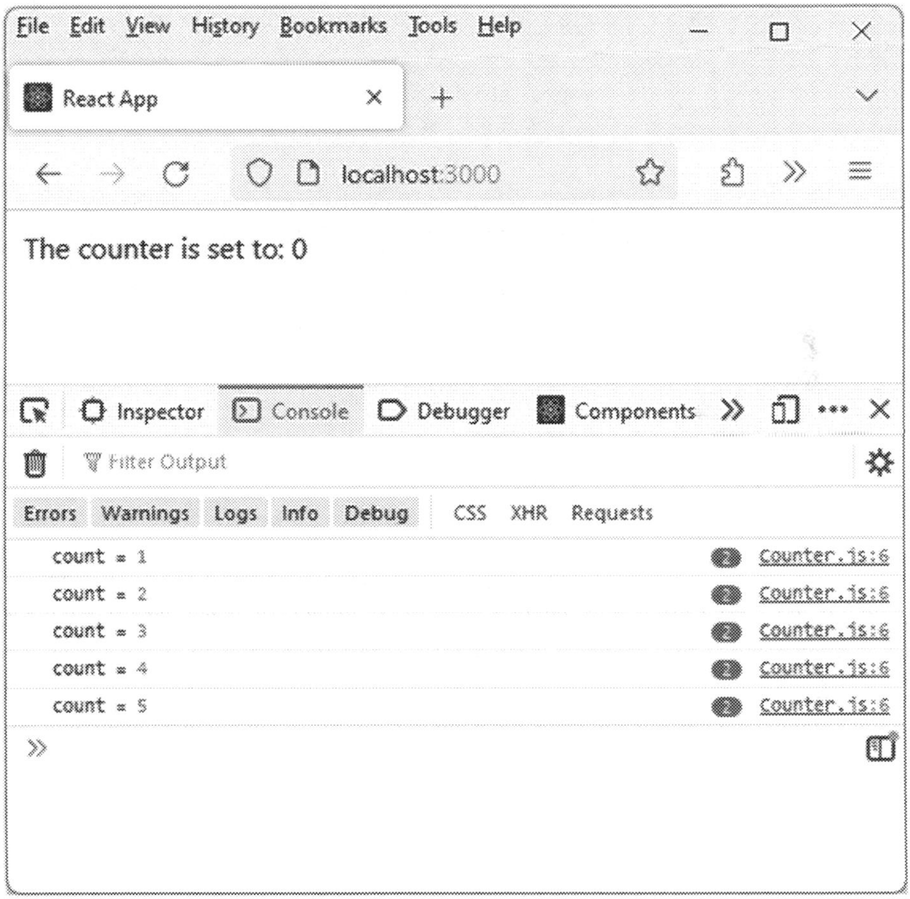

Figure 1-12. Incrementing the counter

Each line is displayed twice in the console, hence the number 2 displayed on the right for each line in the console. This is due to the use of React's strict mode, using the <React.StrictMode> tag in the index.js file. To stop using this strict mode, simply remove the <React.StrictMode> tag surrounding the <App/> tag in the index.js file.

We remove the <React.StrictMode> tag in the index.js file, which becomes as follows:

File src/index.js

```
import React from 'react';
import ReactDOM from 'react-dom/client';
import './index.css';
import App from './App';
import reportWebVitals from './reportWebVitals';

const root = ReactDOM.createRoot(document.
getElementById('root'));
root.render(
  <App />
);

// If you want to start measuring performance in your app, pass
    a function
// to log results (for example: reportWebVitals(console.log))
// or send to an analytics endpoint. Learn more:
    https://bit.ly/CRA-vitals
    reportWebVitals();
```

Now let's observe the values displayed in the browser window and in the console. We can see that the value of the counter increments in the console, but the display in the browser window remains at 0.

This is normal. To change the value of the "count" variable in the displayed page, the "count" variable must be defined as a reactive variable. Only reactive variables can be modified in the display, once the component is rendered.

For this purpose, React uses a concept called "state". The state in a component represents the set of reactive variables defined in that component.

To define a reactive variable in a component, we use the useState() method defined in React. Let's now see how to use the useState() method in a component.

Step 3: Using the useState( ) Method in a Component

The useState() method allows us to define a reactive variable. A reactive variable will be used to display a value in the HTML page, and since the variable is reactive, it can be modified later in the display.

Modifying the value of the reactive variable in the program will automatically update its display. Note that if the variable is not reactive, changing its value will not affect the display.

When a reactive variable is modified in a component, the entire component is re-rendered. The delay between modifying the reactive variable and re-rendering the component is managed by React, and although it's very short, it's not instantaneous.

The modification of reactive variables in the display is carried out during the reconciliation process we mentioned earlier.

The useState() method, used to define a reactive variable, is called a "hook". We will see later that React defines other hooks that will be useful in our programs.

To use the useState() method in a component, simply import it from the "react" module defined in React. The useState() method is indeed exported by the standard "react" module and can be used in a component.

Using the useState() method (file src/Counter.js)

```
import { useState } from "react";

function Counter() {
  const [count, setCount] = useState(0);
```

```
setInterval(function() {
  setCount(count+1);
  console.log("count =", count);
}, 1000);

return (
  <>
  The counter is set to: {count}
  </>
)
}

export default Counter;
```

Now let's explain the previous code:

The import statement allows access to the useState() method defined in the "react" module.

The useState(initValue) method is used to define a reactive variable with an initial value of initValue. The useState() method returns an array containing two values:

- The first value corresponds to the name of the reactive variable. In this case, the reactive variable will be named count, and its initial value will be the one specified in the parameter of the useState(0) call, which is 0.

- The second value corresponds to an update function for the reactive variable. The update function will be named setCount(). Therefore, we will use this update function and never a simple assignment like count = count + 1, which won't work properly with React. This is why the previous display never changed even when the "count" variable was incremented.

In summary, the "count" variable is read-only. It can only be modified using the setCount(newValue) function. This allows React to update the displayed component, which wouldn't be possible by directly updating the "count" variable.

Note that when writing the statement [count, setCount] = useState(0), this is a JavaScript shortcut (called array destructuring). This shortcut is a more concise way of expressing the following three lines of instructions:

Instead of using array destructuring for useState(), you could also write the following:

Equivalent to const [count, setCount] = useState(0);

```
const stateCount = useState(0);
const count = stateCount[0];
const setCount = stateCount[1];
```

It is obviously simpler and faster to use array destructuring allowed by JavaScript rather than the previous lines.

The variable name (here count) and the update function name (here setCount) are arbitrary and chosen by the developer. It is customary to choose the update function name as "set" followed by the name of the reactive variable.

Notice again that the increment of the "count" variable is now performed by setCount(count+1). If you write count++ instead (or count=count+1), it still won't work because the update of the displayed component will not be executed.

Let's see the result obtained in the browser window and also in the console (Figure 1-13).

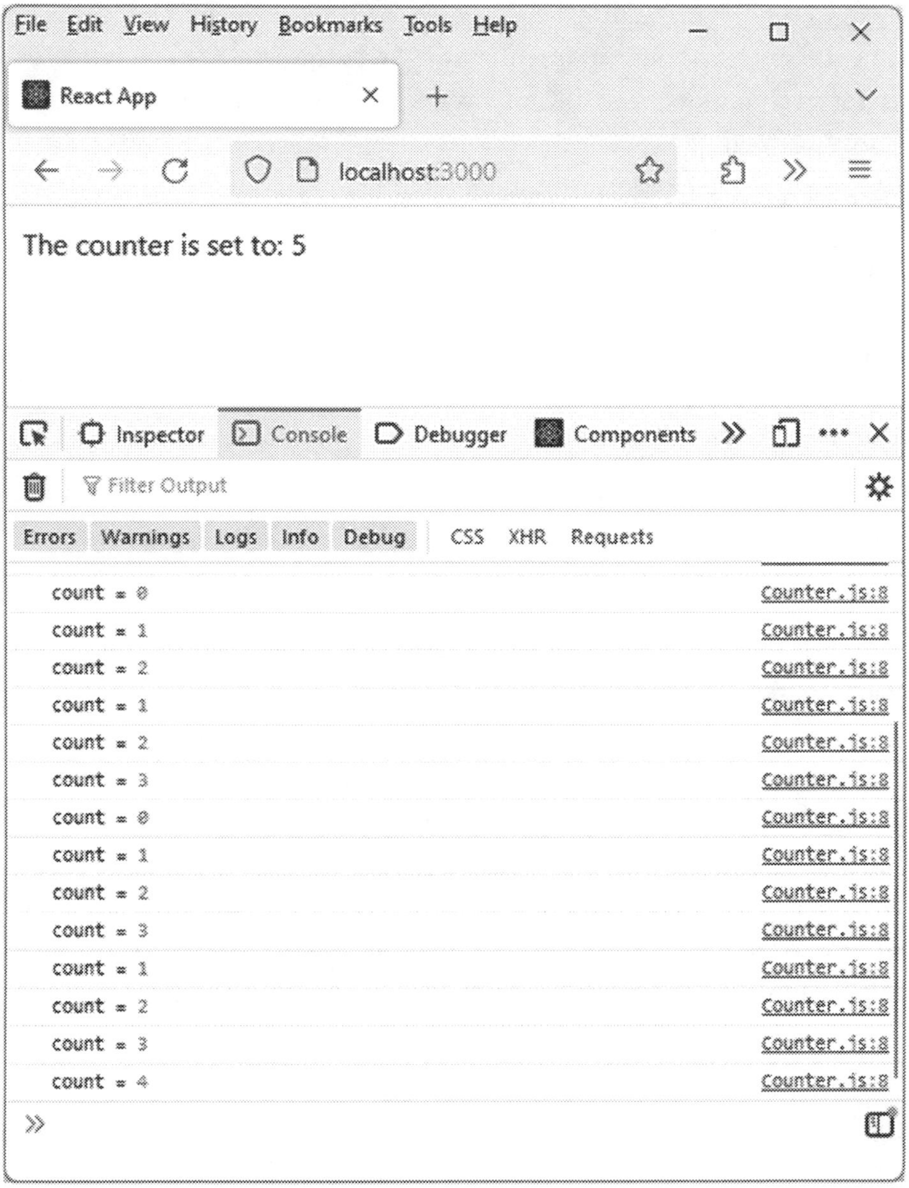

File Edit View History Bookmarks Tools Help   —   □   ✕

■ React App   ✕   +   ⌄

← → C   ○ □ localhost:3000   ☆   ⅀ » ≡

The counter is set to: 5

⌖ ○ Inspector ▣ Console ▢ Debugger ■ Components » ⛶ ••• ✕

🗑 ▽ Filter Output   ⚙

Errors Warnings Logs Info Debug   CSS XHR Requests

count = 0	Counter.js:8
count = 1	Counter.js:8
count = 2	Counter.js:8
count = 1	Counter.js:8
count = 2	Counter.js:8
count = 3	Counter.js:8
count = 0	Counter.js:8
count = 1	Counter.js:8
count = 2	Counter.js:8
count = 3	Counter.js:8
count = 1	Counter.js:8
count = 2	Counter.js:8
count = 3	Counter.js:8
count = 4	Counter.js:8

»   ⬚

Figure 1-13. *Using useState()*

After a certain period of time, a malfunction in the display is observed, which is also visible in the console through the repetitive display of the "count" variable's value.

Indeed, the setCount() function updates the reactive variable, which triggers the new display of the Counter component.

With each modification of the reactive variable "count", the Counter component updates and the Counter() function is executed again. This initiates the start of a new timer by executing the setInterval() instruction.

As a result, the setInterval() function is executed again, causing the counter to be displayed multiple times simultaneously. The timer set by setInterval() should be cleared before the reactive variable "count" is updated. The timer will be restarted during the next component display.

React has provided a way to perform a treatment at the end of component initialization (the first display) or before or after each update (subsequent displays, when a reactive variable of the component is modified). We use the useEffect() method, a new hook defined by React, to achieve this. Let's see how to use useEffect() in our example.

Step 4: Using the useEffect( ) Method in a Component

The useEffect(callback) method defined by React allows you to group a set of instructions to be executed during each display of a component:

- Either during the first display

- Or during subsequent updates, in the case where a reactive variable defined by useState() is modified

The treatments to be performed during each component update are indicated in the callback function used as a parameter for useEffect().

Furthermore, the useEffect() method allows for performing a treatment before each display (i.e., before the component is updated). This is what we're interested in here, as we need to clear the timer before updating the counter in the HTML page.

To perform a treatment before each component update, it is sufficient for the useEffect() method to return a callback function. The treatment indicated in the callback function returned by useEffect() will be executed before each component update.

Let's use the useEffect() method to clear the timer before each counter display.

Using the useEffect() method (file src/Counter.js)

```
import { useState, useEffect } from "react";

function Counter() {
  const [count, setCount] = useState(0);

  useEffect(function() {
    var timer = setInterval(function() {
      setCount(count+1);
      console.log("count =", count);
    }, 1000);

    // If a function is returned by useEffect(),
    // it allows performing a treatment
    // before each component update
    return function() {
      clearInterval(timer);
    }
  });
```

```
  return (
    <>
    The counter is set to: {count}
    </>
  )
}
```

```
export default Counter;
```

Let's explain the previous lines of code:

The useEffect() method is imported from the "react" module, making it usable in the component.

We incorporate the setInterval() method within the callback function of the useEffect(callback) method. We retrieve the value of the timer returned by setInterval() so that we can use this timer argument in the clearInterval(timer) function call.

Note that the clearInterval() function is used within the callback function returned by useEffect(). This ensures that the timer is cleared before the component is updated. The timer will be reactivated in the subsequent component update.

Let's verify that the counter is now functioning correctly (see Figure 1-14).

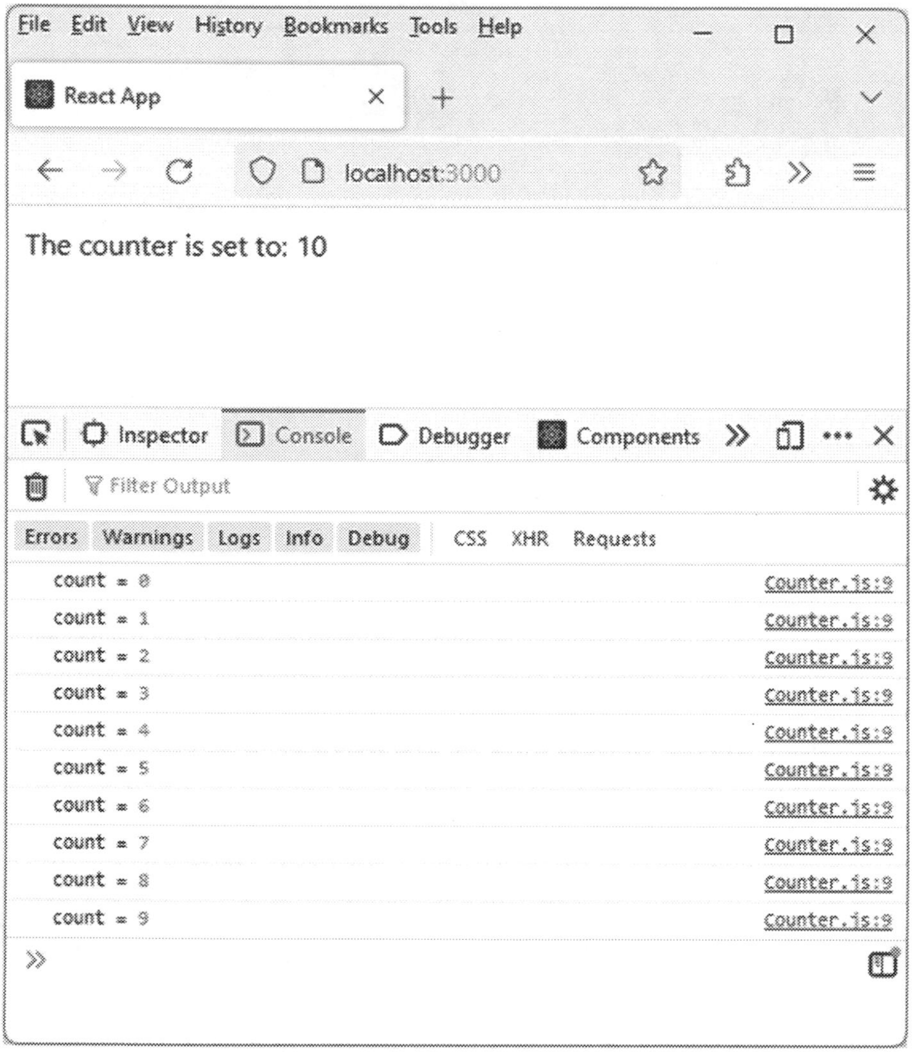

Figure 1-14. *Using useEffect()*

The counter increments gradually. However, there is a mismatch between the value displayed on the page (here the value 10) and the one shown in the console (here the value 9). This is due to the fact that updating the reactive variable "count" using the "setCount(value)" statement is not immediate but asynchronous.

We can verify this by updating the value of "count" twice successively within the useEffect() function.

Double increment of "count" in useEffect() (file src/Counter.js)

```
import { useState, useEffect } from "react";

function Counter() {
  const [count, setCount] = useState(0);

  useEffect(function() {
    var timer = setInterval(function() {
      setCount(count+1);   // 1st increment
      setCount(count+1);   // 2nd increment
      console.log("count =", count);
    }, 1000);

    // If a function is returned by useEffect(),
    // it allows performing a treatment
    // before each component update
    return function() {
      clearInterval(timer);
    }
  });

  return (
    <>
    The counter is set to: {count}
    </>
  )
}

export default Counter;
```

One might expect the counter to increment by 2 every second. However, as shown in Figure 1-15, the counter only increments by 1.

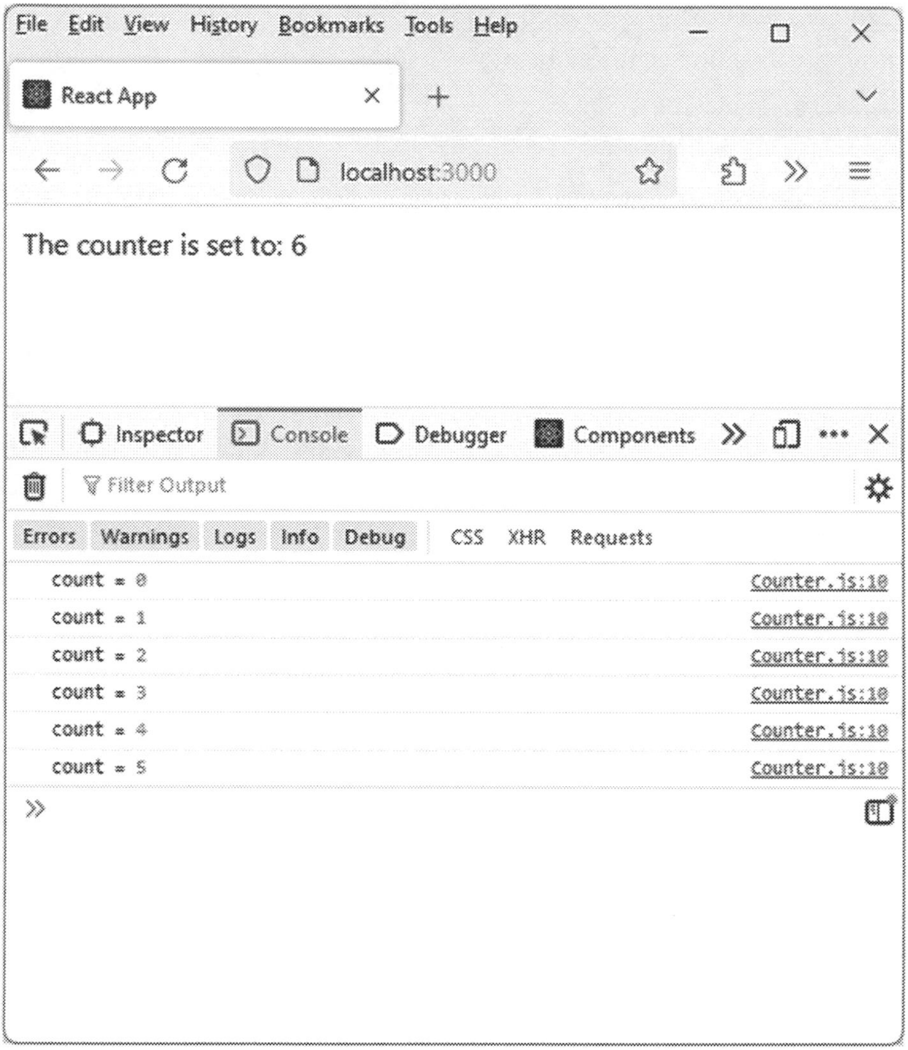

File   Edit   View   History   Bookmarks   Tools   Help   —   □   ✕

■ React App   ✕   +   ∨

←   →   C   ○   ▯   localhost:3000   ☆   ⅀   »   ≡

The counter is set to: 6

▷ | ○ Inspector   ▷ Console   ▯ Debugger   ■ Components   »   ⟋   •••   ✕

🗑   ▽ Filter Output   ✿

Errors **Warnings** **Logs** **Info** **Debug**   CSS   XHR   Requests

  count = 0   Counter.js:10
  count = 1   Counter.js:10
  count = 2   Counter.js:10
  count = 3   Counter.js:10
  count = 4   Counter.js:10
  count = 5   Counter.js:10

»   ⧉

Figure 1-15. *The counter increments by 1 instead of 2 every second*

The reason for the increment of 1 instead of 2 is that, during the second call to setCount(), we are using a value of the "count" variable that is not the latest updated value. Thus, the second increment uses a value of "count" that is not the one obtained as a result of the update during the first increment, but rather the one obtained during the initialization of the callback function.

To handle these cases where we need the latest value of the reactive variable, we use another form of the setCount() function that takes a callback function as a parameter, in the form setCount(callback), instead of the setCount(value) form. The callback function has the form callback(value), where value is the current value of the variable. The callback function should return the new value of the variable (calculated from the current value value passed as a parameter).

We write it like this:

Using the setCount(callback) function (file src/Counter.js)

```
import { useState, useEffect } from "react";

function Counter() {
  const [count, setCount] = useState(0);

  useEffect(function() {
    var timer = setInterval(function() {
      // Instead of:
      // setCount(count+1);   // 1st increment
      // setCount(count+1);   // 2nd increment
      // We write:
      setCount((count)=>count+1);   // 1st increment
      setCount((count)=>count+1);   // 2nd increment
      console.log("count =", count);
    }, 1000);

    // If a function is returned by useEffect(),
    // it allows performing a treatment
    // before each component update
    return function() {
```

```
      clearInterval(timer);
    }
  });

  return (
    <>
    The counter is set to: {count}
    </>
  )
}

export default Counter;
```

The "count" parameter of the callback function here represents the current value of the "count" variable. The callback function here returns count+1. This returned value is used in the second call to setCount(), which thus uses the value that was updated during the first call to setCount().

We can see in Figure 1-16 that the counter is now incremented by 2 every second.

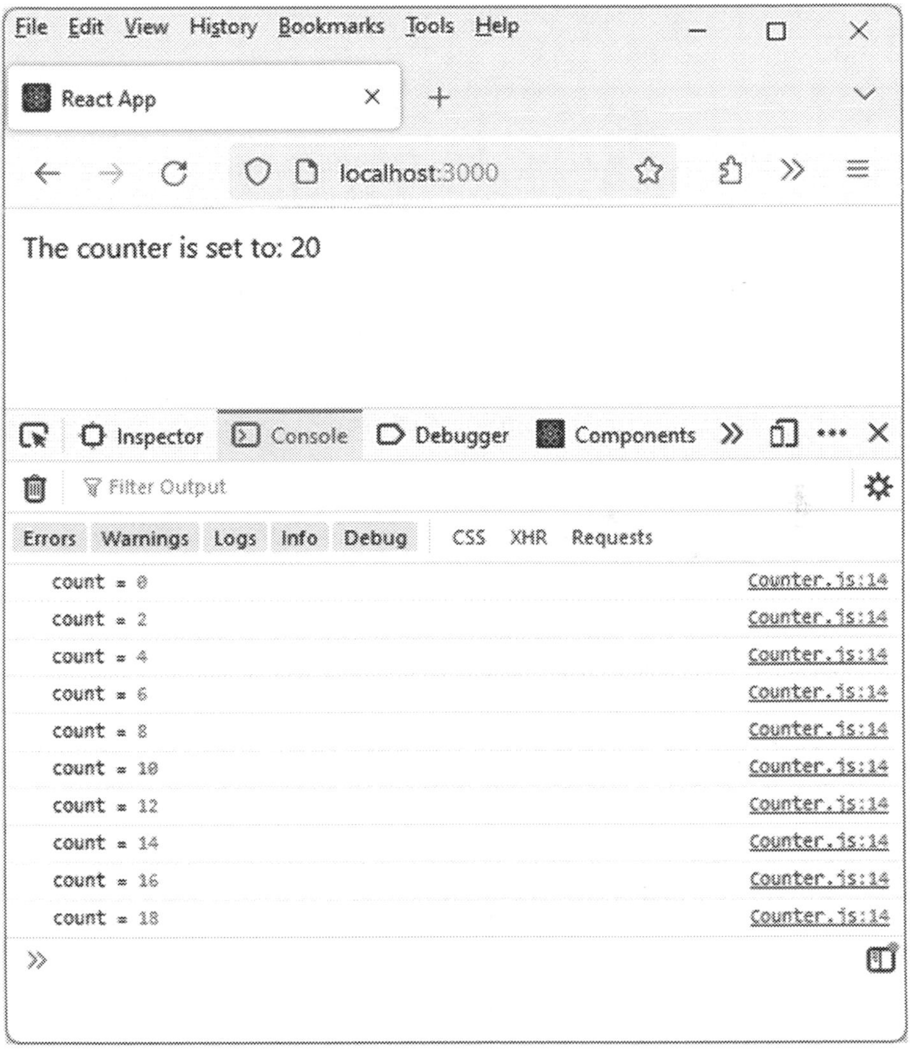

Figure 1-16. *The counter is incremented by 2 every second*

Using a callback function to update a reactive variable (via setCount(callback)) is necessary when the variable update is performed within a callback function such as the one used by useEffect(callback). This approach allows us to use the most recent value of the reactive variable, rather than an old value.

Let's now look at how it's possible to pass parameters to components. For this purpose, we use attributes, also known as props.

Step 5: Using Attributes in Components

It's possible to pass parameters to a component. Each parameter is defined as an attribute in the component. We also use the term property to designate them. We will see how to write it in the following text.

Consider the previous Counter component, for which we want to specify an initial value to start counting, instead of the value 0 as before. We use the attribute "init" (or any other name) for this purpose. The value of the "init" attribute of the Counter component is then written in the App component in one of the following forms:

- As a string (enclosed in single or double quotes)

- As a JavaScript value (enclosed in curly braces { and })

Using the value of the "init" attribute as a string (file src/App.js)

```
<Counter init="5" />
```

Using the value of the "init" attribute as a JavaScript value (file src/App.js)

```
<Counter init={5} />
```

If we don't use the "init" attribute in writing the Counter component, consider that the value of the attribute will be replaced by the value 0. This will provide more flexibility when using the Counter component.

Without using the "init" attribute, which will default to 0 (file src/App.js)

```
<Counter />
```

Let's see how to achieve this by writing the Counter component as follows. Attributes are passed as parameters in the component's creation function, in the form of an object (here named "props", meaning properties or attributes).

The Counter component becomes as follows:

Taking into account the "init" attribute in the component (file src/ Counter.js)

```
import { useState, useEffect } from "react";

function Counter(props) {
  var init = parseInt(props.init || 0);
  const [count, setCount] = useState(init);

  useEffect(function() {
    var timer = setInterval(function() {
      setCount((count)=>count+1);
    }, 1000);

    return function() {
      clearInterval(timer);
    }
  });

  return (
```

```
    <>
      Initial value of the counter is: {init}
      <br />
      The counter is: {count}
    </>
  )
}
```

```
export default Counter;
```

The Counter() function that defines the component now includes the "props" parameter, making it Counter(props). This allows access to the value props.init within the component's body, thereby accessing the value of the "init" attribute used in the Counter component.

The value props.init is used to initialize the initial value of the reactive variable "count" in the state, instead of the value 0 as before, by writing the following:

Initializing the counter with the "init" variable

```
const [count, setCount] = useState(init);
```

We also use the parseInt(props.init) function to retrieve the specified "init" value as an integer; otherwise, we would get a value as a string if written in the form <Counter init="5" />. The statement props.init || 0 initializes to the value 0 if the "init" attribute is not present when using the component.

Note that if we write <Counter init={5} /> using a JavaScript value within curly braces, the parseInt() function becomes optional (and even unnecessary) in this case, as the value 5 is passed to the component, not the string "5".

Let's modify the App.js file of the App component to use the different forms of writing the "init" attribute of the Counter component. We will insert multiple Counter components on the page, each initialized to a different value.

Using the Counter component with the "init" attribute (file src/App.js)

```
import logo from './logo.svg';
import './App.css';
import Counter from "./Counter.js";

function App() {
  return (
    <>
      Counter defined by {"<Counter init='10'/>"}  : <br />
      <Counter init='10' /> <br /> <br />
      Counter defined by {"<Counter init={5} />"} : <br />
      <Counter init={5} /> <br /> <br />
      Counter defined by {"<Counter />"} : <br /> <Counter />
      <br />
    </>
  )
}

export default App;
```

Note that in the JSX code returned by the component, we write a string surrounded by curly braces (like {"<Counter />"}), because to interpret a string containing a component as a string within JSX code, it needs to be enclosed in curly braces (otherwise, it would be replaced with the HTML code of the component).

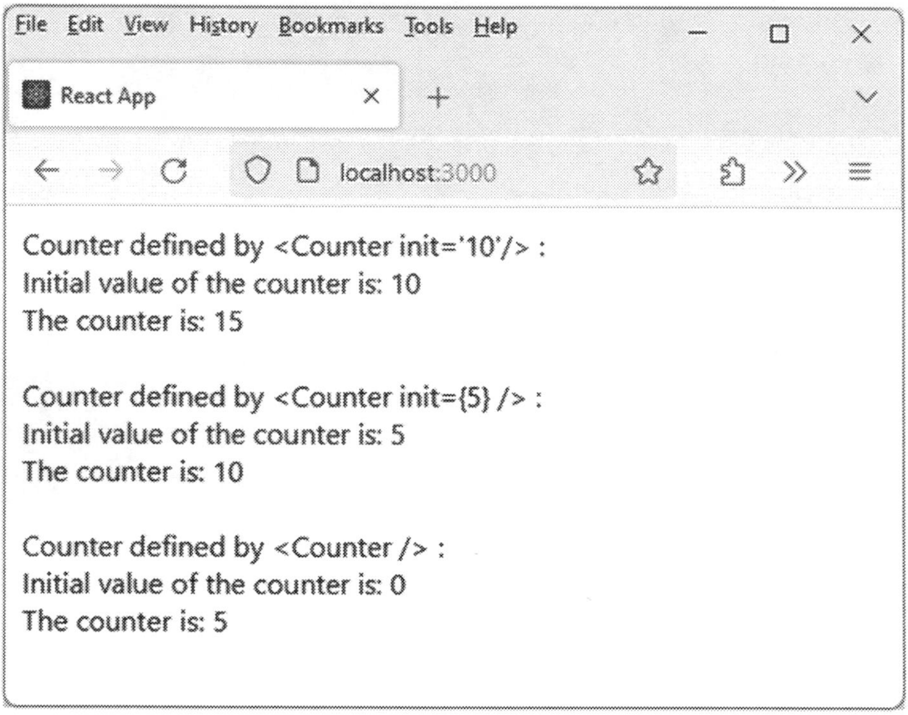

Figure 1-17. *Using attributes in a component*

As seen in Figure 1-17, the various forms of attribute value writing are correctly handled, producing the expected results.

It's common to use ES6 syntax by specifying the component attributes as named properties of a JavaScript object.

Instead of writing

First form of writing (without using ES6 syntax)

```
function Counter(props) {
  var init = parseInt(props.init || 0);
```

One can also write, in an even more readable way

Second form of writing (using ES6 syntax)

```
function Counter({init}) {
  init = parseInt(init || 0);
```

Using the attributes in the form of an object {init} instead of the props parameter allows us to directly use them within the component. Therefore, we write init instead of props.init when using the "init" attribute in the component.

Conclusion

The first day of our React learning journey was dedicated to creating React components. We learned that components are the fundamental building blocks of React, enabling us to create reusable and modular user interfaces. We also discovered how to create a React component using JSX syntax and how the component's properties and state can be leveraged to make our user interface dynamic.

Lastly, we witnessed how React is a flexible and powerful library for crafting dynamic and responsive user interfaces. We are ready to continue our journey with React and further explore key concepts of this exciting JavaScript library, especially delving into how to write JSX code more effectively within components.

CHAPTER 2

Day 2: Mastering JSX Code Writing in a React Component

In this chapter, we will delve deeper into our understanding of JSX, a syntax used to create React components, by using it to create complex components.

JSX is a syntax extension that allows developers to create React components intuitively and in a readable manner. By using JSX, you can combine HTML and JavaScript to create more sophisticated components tailored to the tasks you want to achieve.

Ready to enhance your React skills? Let's get started!

Using the React.Fragment Component

The JSX code of a React component must have a root element that encapsulates all its descendants; otherwise, a runtime error occurs.

To address this, one could wrap the JSX elements included in the component with an enclosing <div> element. This enclosing <div> element, containing all the HTML elements of the component, will be the one returned by the function that describes the component.

However, this <div> element is artificially added in this case because it's not actually necessary (except for encapsulation to avoid the error).

To avoid the need to use an unnecessary <div> element in JSX code, React has created a special element that serves to encapsulate all elements in this root element. This root element won't be displayed in the HTML code returned by the component. This is the role of the React.Fragment component (also referred to as an element).

The React.Fragment component is used in one of the following three forms:

- Directly by using the <React.Fragment> tag

- Directly by using the <Fragment> tag

- By using the <> tag, which is a shorthand version of the previous two (we had already used this tag in the previous chapter)

Let's see how to use each of these tags in JSX code.

Step 1: Using the <React.Fragment> Tag

Here's how to use the <React.Fragment> tag in the JSX code of a component.

Using the <React.Fragment> tag (file src/App.js)

```
import logo from './logo.svg';
import './App.css';
import Counter from "./Counter.js";
import React from "react";

function App() {
  return (
    <React.Fragment>
```

```
      { /* JSX code of the components returned by the
      component */ }
      Counter defined by {"<Counter init='10'/>"}  : <br />
      <Counter init='10' /> <br /> <br />
      Counter defined by {"<Counter init={5} />"} · <br />
      <Counter init={5} /> <br /> <br />
      Counter defined by {"<Counter />"} : <br /> <Counter />
      <br />
    </React.Fragment>
  )
}

export default App;
```

The React.Fragment component is defined in the "react" module, which needs to be included in order to use this component (hence the import React from "react" statement).

The code placed in comments is surrounded by /* and */ as well as curly braces { and }, as in the line { /* JSX code of the components returned by the component */ }. These curly braces are necessary to indicate that what's inside corresponds to JavaScript code (a comment is indeed JavaScript code).

Note that the comment is written between /* and */ because if // is used, in that case, the closing curly brace } must be on a separate line (otherwise it would be seen as part of the comment and wouldn't be considered to end the JavaScript code).

Step 2: Using the <Fragment> Tag

You can also use the <Fragment> tag, which is synonymous with <React. Fragment>. You would write it as follows:

Using the <Fragment> tag (src/App.js file)

```
import logo from './logo.svg';
import './App.css';
import Counter from "./Counter.js";
// import React from "react";
import {Fragment } from "react";

function App() {
  return (
    <Fragment>
      { /* JSX code of the components returned by the
      component */ }
      Counter defined by {"<Counter init='10'/>"}  : <br />
      <Counter init='10' /> <br /> <br />
      Counter defined by {"<Counter init={5} />"} : <br />
      <Counter init={5} /> <br /> <br />
      Counter defined by {"<Counter />"} : <br /> <Counter />
      <br />
    </Fragment>
  )
}

export default App;
```

We replace the inclusion of the React module with that of the Fragment feature, but since this feature is not the default export in the "react" module, it's necessary to name it by enclosing its name in curly braces, in the form import {Fragment} from "react".

Step 3: Using the <> Tag

Let's write the same code using the <> tag, which is the condensed equivalent of <React.Fragment> or <Fragment>:

Using the <> tag (src/App.js file)

```
import logo from './logo.svg';
import './App.css';
import Counter from "./Counter.js";
// import React from "react";
// import {Fragment } from "react";

function App() {
  return (
    <>
      { /* JSX code of the components returned by the
      component */ }
      Counter defined by {"<Counter init='10'/>"}  : <br />
      <Counter init='10' /> <br /> <br />
      Counter defined by {"<Counter init={5} />"} : <br />
      <Counter init={5} /> <br /> <br />
      Counter defined by {"<Counter />"} : <br /> <Counter />
      <br />
    </>
  )
}

export default App;
```

Inclusion from the "react" module is no longer necessary here since the React.Fragment component is not used directly.

Instead, we will use <> and </> to wrap multiple components. However, it is sometimes necessary to use React.Fragment directly, as we will see in the following texts (in cases where we use the key attribute for an element in a list).

Inserting JavaScript Code into JSX

It's possible to write JavaScript code within JSX, provided that the final result is JSX code. This means that the JavaScript code we write must return JSX code, which will be combined with any existing JSX code. All JSX code will then be transformed into HTML code and displayed in the browser.

The JavaScript code we write must be enclosed in curly braces { and }; otherwise, it will be interpreted as regular HTML code.

Let's see how to write the main forms of instructions in JSX, namely, conditions and processing loops.

Writing a Condition in JSX

First, let's show how to write a conditional test that returns different JSX code depending on whether the condition is true or false.

We'll use the previous counters as an example, adding an "end" attribute to the Counter component to indicate at which value we want the counter to stop. If the "end" attribute is not specified in the component or if it's set to 0, the counter does not stop. The end value of the counter is displayed below it, with the text "Counter in progress" if the counter is running or the text "Counter stopped" if the counter is stopped. This corresponds to the condition that we need to write in JSX.

The App.js file containing the counters is as follows:

Using the end attribute in counters (src/App.js file)

```
import logo from './logo.svg';
import './App.css';
import Counter from "./Counter.js";

function App() {
  return (
```

```
    <>
      { /* JSX code of the components returned by the
      component */ }
      Counter defined by {"<Counter init='5'
      end='10'/>"}   : <br />
      <Counter init='5' end='10' />
      <br /> <br />

      Counter defined by {"<Counter init={5} end={15} />"}
      : <br />
      <Counter init={5} end={15} />
      <br /> <br />

      Counter defined by {"<Counter />"} : <br />
      <Counter />
      <br /> <br />
    </>
  )
}

export default App;
```

The first counter goes from 5 to 10, the second from 5 to 15, and the third from 0 to infinity.

The Counter component is modified to take into account the "end" attribute. This can be done using one of the following two methods:

- Either by using an immediately invoked JavaScript function

- Or by using the JavaScript ternary operator

Let's first use an immediately invoked JavaScript function.

Step 1: Using an Immediately Invoked JavaScript Function to Write the Conditional Test

The first way to write the condition is to integrate it into an immediately invoked JavaScript function. Calling the function immediately generates the JSX code to be used.

Considering the "end" attribute in the Counter component (src/ Counter.js file)

```
import { useState, useEffect } from "react";

function Counter({init, end}) {
  init = parseInt(init || 0);
  end = parseInt(end || 0);
  const [count, setCount] = useState(init);

  useEffect(function() {
    if (end && count >= end) return;
    var timer = setInterval(function() {
      setCount((count)=>count+1);
    }, 1000);

    return function() {
      clearInterval(timer);
    }
  });

  return (
    <>
      Initial value of the counter is: {init}
      <br />
      End of the counter at: {end}
```

```
      <br />
      The counter is: {count}
      <br />
      {
        (function(){
          if (end && count >= end) return <b>Counter stopped</b>;
          else return <i>Counter in progress</i>;
        })()
      }
    </>
  )
}

export default Counter;
```

Let's explain these few lines of code here:

We provide the { init, end } component parameters for the two attributes, init and end, used by the component. The value of end is then displayed in the JSX code of the component.

We display the text "Counter stopped" or "Counter in progress" based on whether the current value of the counter (variable count) is greater than or equal to end or not.

The interesting part involves writing the conditional test. It is integrated into an immediately executed JavaScript function (hence the () at the end of it). Indeed, the JSX code displayed in the component must be the result of one or more JavaScript instructions, which is why an immediately invoked function is used here (which in turn returns the JSX code).

After a few seconds, the first two counters are stopped while the third one continues indefinitely (see Figure 2-1).

```
File  Edit  View  History  Bookmarks  Tools  Help          —    □    ✕

■ React App                    ✕    +                            ∨

←  →  C      ○  □  localhost:3000          ☆   ⌖   »   ≡

Counter defined by <Counter init='5' end='10'/> :
Initial value of the counter is: 5
End of the counter at: 10
The counter is: 10
Counter stopped

Counter defined by <Counter init={5} end={15} /> :
Initial value of the counter is: 5
End of the counter at: 15
The counter is: 15
Counter stopped

Counter defined by <Counter /> :
Initial value of the counter is: 0
End of the counter at: 0
The counter is: 200
Counter in progress
```

Figure 2-1. *Using a conditional test to display JSX code*

Note that the immediately invoked function, which returns JSX code, can be replaced by a simple test written in the following form using the JavaScript ternary operator, denoted by a question mark. Let's examine this now.

Step 2: Using the JavaScript Ternary Operator to Write the Conditional Test

The second form of writing a conditional test involves using the JavaScript ternary operator. It is written in the following form:

Using the JavaScript ternary operator

```
condition ? Statement 1 : Statement 2
```

Statement 1 is executed if the condition is true, while statement 2 is executed if the condition is false.

The conditional test previously written using an immediately invoked function (see previous section) can then be written as follows:

Writing a test with the ? operator (called the ternary operator) (src/ Counter.js file)

```
(end && count >= end) ? <b>Counter stopped</b> : <i>Counter in progress</i>
```

If the expressed condition is true, the result of the block of instructions is the first JSX code written (the one after the ? but before the :); otherwise, it's the second one (after the :).

The Counter component file becomes as follows:

Counter component using the ternary operator (src/Counter.js file)

```javascript
import { useState, useEffect } from "react";

function Counter({init, end}) {
  init = parseInt(init || 0);
  end = parseInt(end || 0);
  const [count, setCount] = useState(init);

  useEffect(function() {
    if (end && count >= end) return;
```

61

```
  var timer = setInterval(function() {
    setCount((count)=>count+1);
  }, 1000);

  return function() {
    clearInterval(timer);
  }
});

return (
  <>
    Initial value of the counter is: {init}
    <br />
    End of the counter at: {end}
    <br />
    The counter is: {count}
    <br />
    {
      (end && count >= end) ? <b>Counter stopped</b> :
      <i>Counter in progress</i>
    }
  </>
)
}

export default Counter;
```

This second form of writing (with the ternary operator rather than immediately invoked function) is the most commonly used as it's the simplest to write.

To obtain JSX instructions as a result of a conditional test, never directly use an if(condition) statement in a block of JavaScript code that is not encapsulated in an immediately invoked function; otherwise, there is no way to return the result.

We have seen how to write conditions, now let's explore how to perform processing loops.

Writing a Loop in JSX

Continuing our study of JSX, let's demonstrate how to write a loop that returns JSX code.

We want to display three counters (each associated with the Counter component) using a loop in JSX. Each counter starts and ends with the following values:

- The first counter starts at 5 and ends at 10. This is equivalent to a JSX instruction of the form <Counter init="5" end="10" />.

- The second counter starts at 5 and ends at 11. This is equivalent to a JSX instruction of the form <Counter init="5" end="11" />.

- The third counter starts at 5 and ends at 12. This is equivalent to a JSX instruction of the form <Counter init="5" end="12" />.

Here, we're looping through three counters, but you could create a loop for a larger number of elements.

To write the loop of JSX instructions, there are several possible approaches that we'll explain in the following texts:

- Using an immediately invoked function

- Using the map() method of the JavaScript Array class

Let's begin by explaining this using the first solution, which involves using an immediately invoked function to write the loop of JSX instructions.

Step 1: Writing the JSX Loop Using an Immediately Invoked Function

As we saw when writing the conditional test, it's possible to produce JSX code using an immediately invoked function. We wrap this function in curly braces { and }.

Since the App.js file displays the Counter components, it is this file that is modified to write the loop of JSX instructions that display the counters.

Display three Counter components using an immediately invoked function (file src/App.js)

```
import logo from './logo.svg';
import './App.css';
import Counter from "./Counter.js";

function App() {
  return (
    <>
      {
        (function() {
          var jsx = [];
          for (var i=0; i<3; i++) {
            jsx.push(
              <>
                Counter {i} defined by {`<Counter init='5'
                end='${10+i}' />`}  : <br />
                <Counter init='5' end={10+i} />
                <br/><br/>
              </>
            );
          }
```

```
        return jsx;
      })()
    }
  </>
  )
}
```

```
export default App;
```

The variable jsx (of the Array class) in the immediately invoked function is initialized to an empty array. This variable is used to accumulate the JSX instructions that will be returned by the function. JSX instructions are accumulated in the jsx array variable using the jsx. push() method. The end attribute indicating the end value of the counter corresponds to 10+0 for the first counter, 10+1 for the second, and 10+2 for the third.

Notice the use of backticks ` and ` to open and close a string and the use of JavaScript expressions in the form ${val} to incorporate the value of the val variable into the string.

After running the program and stopping the first and second counters, the displayed page is shown in Figure 2-2.

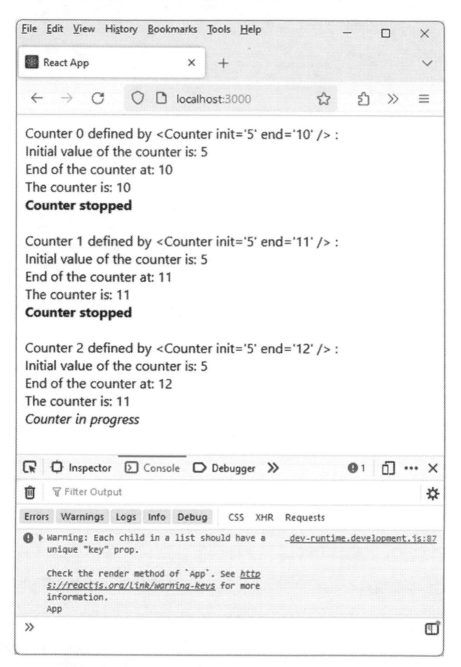

Figure 2-2. *Counters displayed by a loop*

Although the program is functioning correctly, we intentionally display the console window (by pressing the F12 key on the keyboard) because this window contains valuable information. React recommends adding a special attribute called key for each JSX element displayed via a loop. This key attribute, whose value must be unique for each JSX element displayed in the loop, allows React to handle long lists more efficiently.

Let's immediately see how to take this valuable advice from React into account, by showing how to use the key attribute in JSX elements displayed by a loop.

Step 2: Using the "key" Attribute in JSX Elements Displayed by a Loop

Let's see how to integrate the key attribute into each element displayed in the list.

Using the key attribute to display each element of the list (src/App.js file)

```
import logo from './logo.svg';
import './App.css';
import Counter from "./Counter.js";
import React from "react";

function App() {
  return (
    <>
      {
        (function() {
          var jsx = [];
          for (var i=0; i<3; i++) {
            jsx.push(
              <React.Fragment key={i}>
```

```
                Counter {i} defined by {`<Counter init='5'
                end='${10+i}' />`}  : <br />
                <Counter init='5' end={10+i} />
                <br/><br/>
              </React.Fragment>
            );
          }
          return jsx;
        })()
      }
    </>
  )
}

export default App;
```

The key attribute can be placed on any JSX element except the one defined by and terminated by. However, you can replace this element with its equivalent <React.Fragment>, provided you import the React object defined in the "react" module (hence the import React from "react" statement).

You can verify that the list now displays in the same way, but without any error messages in the console.

Step 3: Important Rule About the Value of the "key" Attribute in List Elements

The value of each key attribute must be unique in the list, and each list element must always retain the same value for its key attribute (the one previously assigned to it), or errors may occur.

For example, if you use the index of the element in the list as the value of the key attribute, this could lead to potential errors. The index of an inserted element might be the same as that of a previously deleted element. This would cause an error because two different elements would have had the same key attribute value in the list.

It's also important that each list element always maintains its same key attribute value. If the key attribute is changed for an element, React will treat it as a new element and re-create it, which can impact performance and cause state and rendering issues.

In summary, by following these rules of unique and stable keys, React can efficiently optimize the update of list elements, ensuring optimal performance and preventing display errors.

Step 4: Writing the JSX Loop Using the map( ) Method of the JavaScript Array Class

Now that we've covered the main rules for correctly using the key attribute in lists of JSX elements, let's explore the second way to write a loop of JSX instructions using the map() method of the JavaScript Array class.

Indeed, the map() method of the JavaScript Array class is also commonly used for loops that return blocks of JSX code.

The map(callback) method is used on an array, and for each element in this array, the callback(elem) function is used to return a new element that will replace elem in the final array returned by the map() method.

The map() method allows you to construct a new array from the initial array. In all cases, the new array will contain the same number of elements as the initial array (in contrast, for example, to the filter() method of the JavaScript Array class, which can return fewer elements than in the initial array).

Let's use the same example as before, where we displayed three counters with different end values.

Instead of using an immediately invoked function as before, let's now use the map() method to loop from 0 to 2 inclusive. The map() method will return each list element that will be displayed:

Using the map() method to create the list in JSX (src/App.js file)

```
import logo from './logo.svg';
import './App.css';
import Counter from "./Counter.js";
import React from "react";

function App() {
  return (
    <>
      {
        [0, 1, 2].map(function(i) {
          return (
            <React.Fragment key={i}>
              Counter {i} defined by {`<Counter init='5'
              end='${10+i}' />`}   : <br/>
              <Counter init='5' end={10+i} />
              <br/><br/>
            </React.Fragment>
          )
        })
      }
    </>
  )
}

export default App;
```

Each element of the initial array [0, 1, 2] is passed to the callback function indicated in the map(callback) method. The callback function returns a block of JSX code (the same one we constructed in the previous section with a for loop). The new array constructed as a result of the map() method call will be used to display the App component

Of course, we're using the React.Fragment component with the key attribute, as explained in the previous sections.

Step 5: Using the map( ) Method to Display Large Lists of Elements

Let's now provide some advice for cases where you want to loop using the map() method over a larger number of elements.

We'll explain as follows how to loop over ten elements using the map() method, but the principle is the same for any number of elements.

So, to loop over ten elements, instead of writing an array of ten elements like [0, 1, 2, 3, 4, 5, 6, 7, 8, 9], you can write

Equivalent to [0, 1, 2, 3, 4, 5, 6, 7, 8, 9]

```
[...Array(10).keys()]
```

Indeed, Array(10) creates an array of ten empty elements (with a value of undefined). The keys() method on this array returns an Array Iterator object containing keys for each index of the array (i.e., the values 0, 1, 2, ..., 9 corresponding to the indices in the array). The spread operator ... in front lists these values, while the square brackets [and] transform this result into a JavaScript array.

Finally, if you want to start at 1 instead of 0, you can use the slice() method, like this

Equivalent to [1, 2, 3, 4, 5, 6, 7, 8, 9, 10]

```
[...Array(11).keys()].slice(1)
```

Indeed, the slice(1) method allows you to remove the first element from the array (the one containing the value 0). To obtain a sequence of 10 values, you can create an array of 11 elements and keep only the last 10 by removing the first one.

Using Styles in JSX

To conclude our study of JSX, let's see how to write styles in HTML elements using JSX. For this purpose, we use the style attribute, whose value should be a JavaScript object representing the different style properties and values of the HTML element.

For example, you can specify { color: "red", fontSize: "15px" }.

The CSS font-size property is written here as fontSize (camelCase notation) when writing the style.

Notice that in JSX, you write style={{ color: "red", fontSize: "15px" }}, using double curly braces. The first { indicates that you're using JavaScript code within JSX, while the second { indicates the beginning of the JavaScript object being used.

The Counter component that displays the text "Counter stopped" in red with a font size of 20px then becomes

Displaying a style in a JSX element (src/Counter.js file)

```
import { useState, useEffect } from "react";

function Counter({init, end}) {
  init = parseInt(init || 0);
  end = parseInt(end || 0);
  const [count, setCount] = useState(init);

  useEffect(function() {
    if (end && count >= end) return;
    var timer = setInterval(function() {
```

```
    setCount((count)=>count+1);
  }, 1000);

  return function() {
    clearInterval(timer);
  }
});

return (
  <>
    Initial value of the counter is: {init}
    <br />
    End of the counter at: {end}
    <br />
    The counter is: {count}
    <br />
    {
      (end && count >= end) ? <b style={{color:"red",
      fontSize:"20px"}}>Counter stopped</b> :
                                      <i>Counter in
                                      progress</i>

    }
  </>
  )
}

export default Counter;
```

When the first counter is stopped and the others are still in progress, the display becomes as shown in Figure 2-3.

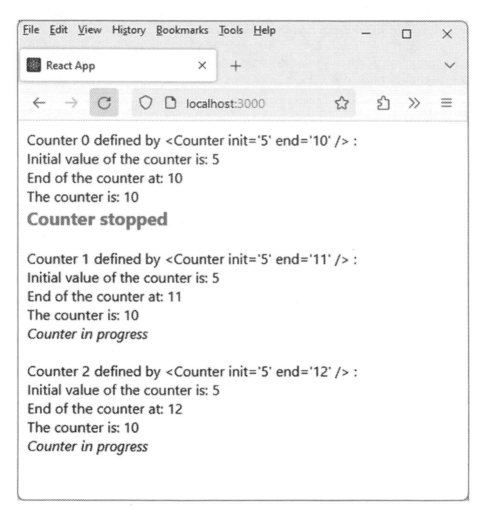

Figure 2-3. *Using a style in a component*

The text "Counter stopped" in the first counter is displayed in red with a font size of 20px.

Conclusion

The second day of our React learning journey was dedicated to writing JSX code within a React component. We learned how to integrate JavaScript code into JSX to make our user interface more dynamic, using conditional tests and processing loops.

We are now ready to continue our learning journey with React and explore further possibilities offered by this exciting JavaScript library, particularly by learning how to manage user interface events.

CHAPTER 3

Day 3: Mastering Event Handling in a React Component

In this chapter, we will learn how to handle events in React components.
Events are actions triggered by the user, such as clicking a button or entering text into a form. In React, you can add event handlers to your elements to control their behavior in response to user actions.

Throughout this chapter, you will learn

- How to handle events in React components
- How to manipulate the state of your application in response to user interface events

Ready to add interactivity to your React applications? Let's get started!

© Eric Sarrion 2023
E. Sarrion, *Master React in 5 Days*, https://doi.org/10.1007/978-1-4842-9855-8_3

Handling Click Events on a Button

Let's begin our study of event handling in React by managing click events on a button within a component. We'll see how to

- Capture the event in the JSX code of the component

- Perform the processing associated with the button click

- Manage reactive variables used within the component

First, let's explore how an event is handled in a React component.

Step 1: Capturing an Event in a React Component

Let's now delve into how React enables event handling within components. Capturing an event is done directly in the JSX code of the component. If you want to learn more or understand JSX code better, refer to the previous chapter, which explains it in detail.

To capture events in JSX code, you use HTML event attributes by converting their names to camelCase in JSX code.

For example, you would use the onClick attribute to handle a click on an HTML element, or onDoubleClick to handle a double-click. These attribute names correspond to the HTML onclick and ondoubleclick attributes.

The value associated with the attribute points to a JavaScript processing function defined in the React component. In the attribute's value, you enclose the function name with curly braces { } (because the function name is treated as a JavaScript expression, hence the surrounding curly braces).

For instance, you would write onClick={handleClick} to have the click processing performed in the handleClick() function. This processing function will be defined within the component and can access reactive variables defined by useState() within the component.

Note that you don't write onClick={handleClick()}. This would mean executing the handleClick() function on every component render, while we want it to be executed only on each button click.

Let's see a few examples of how to handle events in a React component.

Step 2: Incrementing a Counter by Clicking an Increment Button

To learn how to handle events in React components, let's start with something simple.

We want to use the counter from the previous chapter (Counter component) but manage its increment by clicking a "count+1" button, instead of incrementing it periodically every second.

The Counter component is modified to handle the click on the "count+1" button. Here, the increment is no longer performed at regular intervals as before but rather triggered by a click on the "count+1" button.

The modified Counter component, now handling the click on the "count+1" button, is as follows:

Insertion of a button for incrementing the counter (src/Counter.js file)

```
import { useState } from "react";

function Counter({init, end}) {
  init = parseInt(init || 0);
  end = parseInt(end || 0);
  const [count, setCount] = useState(init);
```

```
function incr() {
  setCount((count)=>count+1);
}

return (
  <>
    Initial value of the counter is: {init}
    <br />
    End of the counter at: {end}
    <br />
    The counter is: {count}
    <br />
    {
      (count < end) ?
        <>
          <i>Counter in progress</i> 
          <button onClick={incr}>count+1</button>
        </>:
          <b>Counter stopped</b>
    }
  </>
)
}

export default Counter;
```

Let's emphasize once again on the syntax of the attribute value: you write onClick={incr} and not onClick={incr()}.

Indeed, if you write incr(), it would mean that the function incr() is automatically called every time the component is rendered (because any function call within JSX code is executed during component rendering). To prevent this and ensure that the incr() call only happens upon clicking the button, you simply write {incr}. This way, you're providing a reference to the click event handling function.

The App component responsible for displaying the counters remains the same (it's the same file as in the previous chapter):

App component displaying the three counters (src/App.js file)

```
import logo from './logo.svg';
import './App.css';
import Counter from "./Counter.js";
import React from "react";

function App() {
  return (
    <>
      {
        [0, 1, 2].map(function(i) {
          return (
            <React.Fragment key={i}>
              Counter {i} defined by {`<Counter init='5'
              end='${10+i}' />`}  : <br/>
              <Counter init='5' end={10+i} />
              <br/><br/>
            </React.Fragment>
          )
        })
      }
    </>
  )
}

export default App;
```

By incrementing the first counter to its maximum value (10) through clicking the button, the "count+1" button of that counter disappears (Figure 3-1).

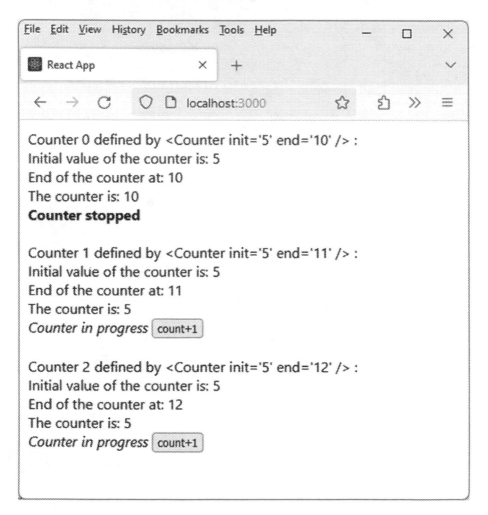

Figure 3-1. *Clicks on the "count+1" button*

The program functions correctly, and clicking the "count+1" buttons produces the expected result.

Now let's look at another example that allows starting a counter, automatically incrementing it by 1 every second.

Step 3: Starting a Periodic Counter by Clicking a Start Button

Instead of clicking the "count+1" button to modify the counter, we now use a Start button that initiates counting until the final value is reached. The Start button disappears when clicked and reappears once the final value is reached, allowing the initiation of a new count.

To achieve this, we utilize a new reactive variable called "start" which indicates whether the Start button should be displayed (start is true) or not (start is false). The Start button is displayed during the initial component rendering (start is initialized to true) and then disappears as soon as the counter begins counting toward its final value (start is set to false).

Counter with Start button (file src/Counter.js)

```
import { useState, useEffect } from "react";

function Counter({init, end}) {
  init = parseInt(init || 0);
  end = parseInt(end || 0);
  const [count, setCount] = useState(init);
  const [start, setStart] = useState(true);   // true for
  displaying the Start button

  useEffect(function() {
    if (!start) {
      // The Start button is not displayed; you can initiate
        the timer.
      var timer = setInterval(function() {
        setCount((count)=>{
          var newCount = count+1;
          if (newCount >= end) setStart(true);
          return newCount;
```

```
        });
      }, 1000);
    }

    return function() {
      clearInterval(timer);
    }
  });

  function restart() {
    setStart(false);   // Hide the Start button
    setCount(init);    // Reset "count" to the initial value.
  }

  return (
    <>
      Initial value of the counter is: {init}
      <br />
      End of the counter at: {end}
      <br />
      The counter is: {count}
      <br />
      {
        (start) ?
          <>
            <b>Counter stopped</b> 
            <button onClick={restart}>Start</button>
          </>:
          <i>Counter in progress</i>
      }
    </>
  )
}

export default Counter;
```

As explained in Chapter 1, we utilize the useEffect() method to perform an action upon component rendering or update. This enables the initiation of the timer, incrementing the counter every second.

The restart() function manages the click on the Start button. It hides the Start button (start is set to false) and resets the counter "count" to the initial value "init".

Upon program launch, the counters are paused and ready to start (Figure 3-2).

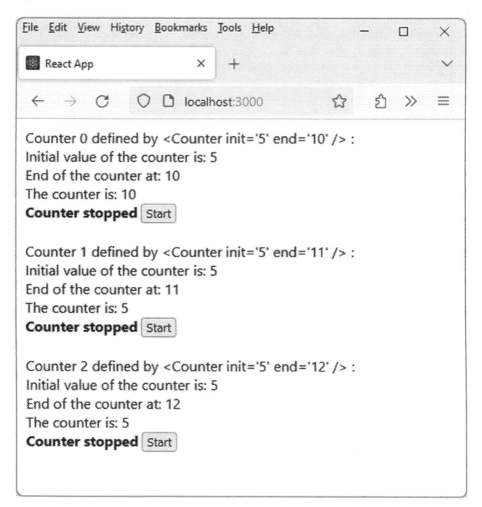

Figure 3-2. *Counters are ready to start*

Let's click the Start button associated with the second counter; it will start counting until it reaches its end value. Here's the display in progress (Figure 3-3).

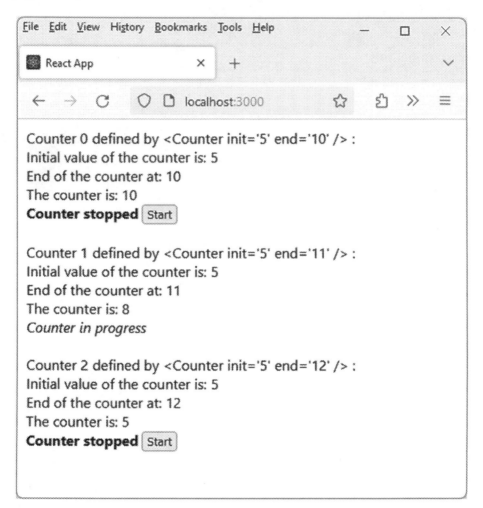

Figure 3-3. *The second counter is in progress*

When the counter reaches the final value (here, 11 for the second counter), the display becomes as shown in Figure 3-4.

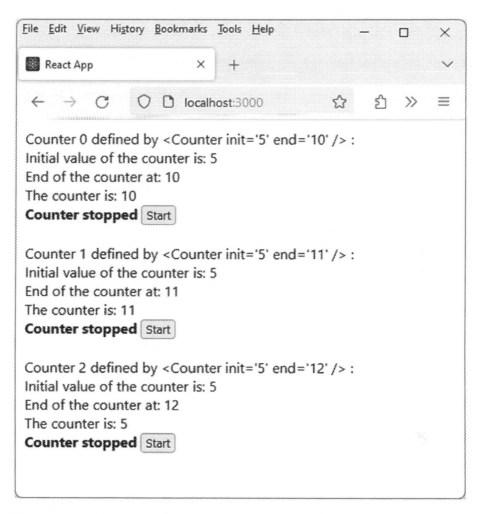

Figure 3-4. *The second counter is now stopped*

Once the counter reaches its maximum value, the Start button is displayed again. Clicking this Start button restarts the counter.

Let's now enhance the program by allowing the counter to start automatically the first time.

Step 4: Automatically Start the Counter the First Time

We want to introduce a new attribute in the Counter component called "autostart". This "autostart" attribute indicates whether we want the counter to start automatically the first time (without needing to click the Start button the first time) or not:

- We'll write autostart="1" to automatically start the counter.

- We'll write autostart="0" to not start the counter automatically.

- If the "autostart" attribute is not specified, it is assumed to have a value of 0.

We want only the first two displayed counters to start automatically, while the following counters will need to be started by clicking their respective Start buttons.

The App component is modified to use the "autostart" attribute in the Counter component.

Using the "autostart" attribute in the Counter components (file src/App.js)

```
import logo from './logo.svg';
import './App.css';
import Counter from "./Counter.js";
import React from "react";
function App() {
  return (
    <>
      {
```

```
      [...Array(3).keys()].map(function(i) {
        var val = i < 2 ? '1' : '0';  // Value of the
        "autostart" attribute
        return (
          <React.Fragment key={i}>
            Counter {i} defined by {`<Counter autostart=
            '${val}' init='5' end='${10+i}' />`}  : <br/>
            <Counter autostart={val} init='5' end={10+i} />
            <br/><br/>
          </React.Fragment>
        )
      })
    }
  </>
  )
}

export default App;
```

The value of the "autostart" attribute is calculated based on the value of the displayed counter's index i.

The Counter component is modified to take the "autostart" attribute into account:

Using the "autostart" attribute in the Counter component (file src/Counter.js)

```
import { useState, useEffect } from "react";

function Counter({init, end, autostart}) {
  init = parseInt(init || 0);
  end = parseInt(end || 0);
  autostart = parseInt(autostart || 0);
  const [count, setCount] = useState(init);
```

```
const [start, setStart] = useState(true);   // true for
displaying the Start button

useEffect(function() {
  if (!start) {
    // The Start button is not displayed; you can initiate
      the timer.
    var timer = setInterval(function() {
      setCount((count)=>{
        var newCount = count+1;
        if (newCount >= end) setStart(true);
        return newCount;
      });
    }, 1000);
  }

  return function() {
    clearInterval(timer);
  }
});

useEffect(function() {
  if (autostart) restart()
}, );

function restart() {
  setStart(false);  // Hide the Start button
  setCount(init);   // Reset "count" to the initial value.
}

return (
  <>
    Initial value of the counter is: {init}
    <br />
```

```
    End of the counter at: {end}
    <br />
    The counter is: {count}
    <br />
    {
      (start) ?
        <>
          <b>Counter stopped</b> 
          <button onClick={restart}>Start</button>
        </> :
        <i>Counter in progress</i>
    }
  </>
 )
}

export default Counter;
```

The "autostart" attribute is integrated into the component's parameters (in addition to the "init" and "end" attributes).

The interesting part of the previous code is the one using the second useEffect() method call. We use a second call to the useEffect() method with an additional parameter, which is an empty array.

Indeed, multiple useEffect() methods can be used within a component. Let's explain the use of the second useEffect() method call:

In addition to executing the provided callback function as a parameter of useEffect(callback) upon component rendering or update, we can also specify conditions under which the callback function will be executed. For instance, we might want to execute it only during the initial rendering of the component (and not for subsequent updates of the component). To achieve this, we provide an empty array as the second parameter of the useEffect() method. This empty array indicates that the callback function should be executed only during the initial rendering of the component.

Thanks to this parameter set to [], the restart() function will be called only when the component is initially rendered and not during its subsequent updates. This behavior aligns with the desired outcome.

Upon program launch, we verify that the first two counters automatically start (with "autostart" set to 1), while the next one waits for the user to click its Start button (Figure 3-5).

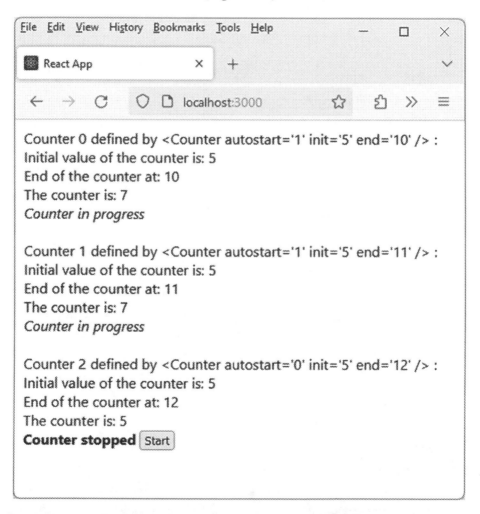

Figure 3-5. *The first two counters start automatically*

In these sections, we have seen how to manage events on a button through several examples. Now, let's explore how to handle other events related to input fields in an HTML page.

Managing the Content of an Input Field

In this example, we simply want to display and manage an input field. The previous counter is replaced with an input field where any value can be entered. The entered value is also displayed below the input field. It updates as the user types.

The App component is modified to incorporate the new Counter component:

App component incorporating the Counter component (file src/App.js)

```
import logo from './logo.svg';
import './App.css';
import Counter from "./Counter.js";
import React from "react";
function App() {
  return (
    <>
      <Counter />
    </>
  )
}

export default App;
```

The Counter component displaying the input field becomes:

Counter component incorporating the input field (file src/Counter.js)

```
import { useState } from "react";

function Counter() {
  const [value, setValue] = useState("");

  function change(event) {
    setValue(event.target.value);
  }

  return (
    <>
      Counter : <input type="text" onChange={change} /> <br/>
      <br/>
      Input Value : {value}
    </>
  )
}

export default Counter;
```

We use a reactive variable "value" to display the value entered in the field on the page. We achieve this using the onChange attribute, which allows us to receive the event indicating that the value of the field has been modified.

Upon receiving the onChange event on the input field, the change() function is triggered. It retrieves the value entered in the field using event. target.value and then sets this value in the reactive variable value using the setValue() method returned by useState().

Let's verify that the displayed value changes as we type in the input field (Figure 3-6).

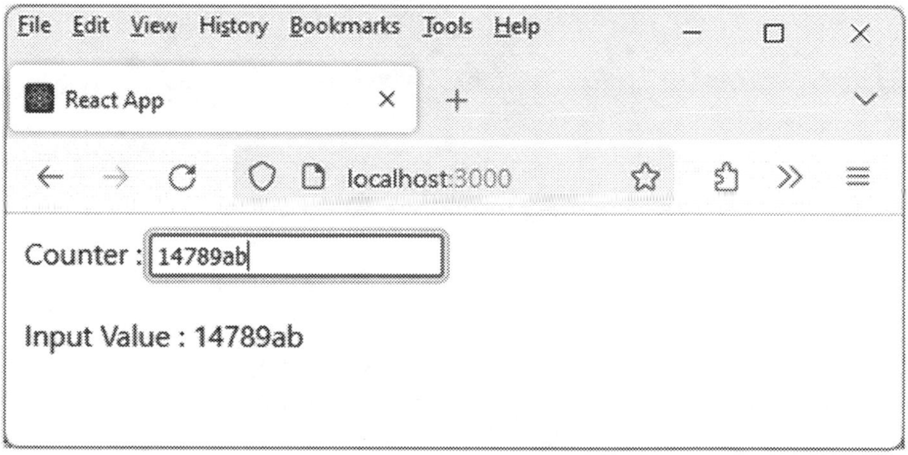

Figure 3-6. *Displaying a value while typing*

Indeed, with each character entered in the input field, the reactive variable displayed on the screen is appropriately updated.

Now, let's see how to improve this program by allowing only digits to be entered in the input field.

Step 1: Allow Only Digits During Input

Let's enhance the previous program by allowing only digits to be entered, as well as allowing movement keys (ArrowLeft, ArrowRight, Tab) and deletion keys (Backspace and Delete). In the previous program, any character could be entered in the input field.

To allow only digits to be entered in the field, we should not use the onChange event, as it detects changes in the field's content but does not filter based on the pressed key. Instead, we will use the onKeyDown attribute, which indicates that a key on the keyboard has been pressed. Depending on the pressed key, we will decide whether that key is accepted or not.

Allow only the entry of digits in the input field (file src/Counter.js)

```
import { useState } from "react";

function Counter() {
  const [value, setValue] = useState("");

  function change(event) {
    setValue(event.target.value);
  }

  function keydown(event) {
    // Display the pressed key in the console
    console.log(event.key);
    // Allow the Backspace, Delete, ArrowLeft, ArrowRight, and
        Tab keys
    if (["Backspace", "Delete", "ArrowLeft", "ArrowRight",
    "Tab"].includes(event.key)) return;
    // Then disallow all other keys except those from 0 to 9
    if (event.key < "0" || event.key > "9") event.
    preventDefault();
  }

  return (
    <>
      Counter : <input type="text" onChange={change}
      onKeyDown={keydown} /> <br/><br/>
      Input Value : {value}
    </>
  )
}

export default Counter;
```

We use the method event.preventDefault() associated with the event object received as a parameter in the function to reject key presses of non-numeric keys. The preventDefault() method is a JavaScript method associated with Event class objects.

We can confirm that only numeric keys and movement keys are being considered in the field.

Step 2: Give Focus to the Input Field upon Component Rendering

Let's enhance the previous program by giving immediate focus to the input field upon component rendering (without needing to click it).

We achieve this using the focus() method defined in JavaScript, which is used on the DOM element that we want to give focus to. To do this, we need to access the DOM element from JavaScript or JSX code.

React introduces the concept of references, simply called refs, to address this. React provides the useRef() method, which returns a reference that can be placed in JSX code using the HTML ref attribute.

Let's modify the Counter component's code to implement focus management using this functionality:

Automatically give focus to the input field (file src/Counter.js)

```
import { useState, useEffect, useRef } from "react";

function Counter() {
  const [value, setValue] = useState("");
  const refCounter = useRef();

  useEffect(function() {
    refCounter.current.focus();  // refCounter.current
    represents the DOM element associated with that reference
  }, );
```

```
function change(event) {
  setValue(event.target.value);
}

function keydown(event) {
  // Display the pressed key in the console
  console.log(event.key);
  // Allow the Backspace, Delete, ArrowLeft, ArrowRight, and
     Tab keys
  if (["Backspace", "Delete", "ArrowLeft", "ArrowRight",
  "Tab"].includes(event.key)) return;
  // Then disallow all other keys except those from 0 to 9
  if (event.key < "0" || event.key > "9") event.
  preventDefault();
}

return (
  <>
    Counter : <input type="text" onChange={change}
    onKeyDown={keydown} ref={refCounter} />
    <br/><br/>
    Input Value : {value}
  </>
)
}

export default Counter;
```

Let's explain the previous code:

First, we obtain a reference named refCounter by using the statement refCounter = useRef(). This refCounter reference is also indicated in the JSX code using the ref attribute, where you write ref={refCounter} within the <input> element. This establishes the connection between the JSX code and the JavaScript code earlier.

Next, we need to be able to give focus to the element referenced by refCounter. To achieve this, we use the useEffect(callback,) method, where we provide an empty array as the second parameter. This empty array signifies that the callback function should only be executed once, after the component is created.

Accessing the referenced DOM element is done via the current property of refCounter, which is refCounter.current. Calling the focus() method on this DOM element gives it focus directly when the component is rendered.

We verify that the input field receives focus immediately upon program launch (Figure 3-7).

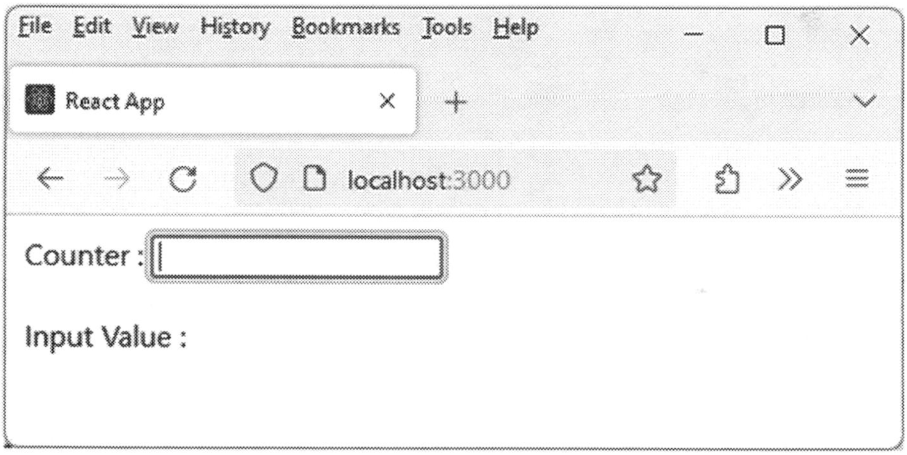

Figure 3-7. *The input field gains focus immediately*

In the following section, we further enhance the program by allowing multiple counters to be displayed, and we display their total sum as digits are entered into the fields.

Step 3: Display Multiple Counters and Show Their Real-Time Sum

Now, we want to display multiple counters and show the total of all counters as digits are entered in the input fields.

For example, with three counters, and entering 10 in the first, 20 in the second, and 30 in the third, a total of 60 will be displayed as in Figure 3-8.

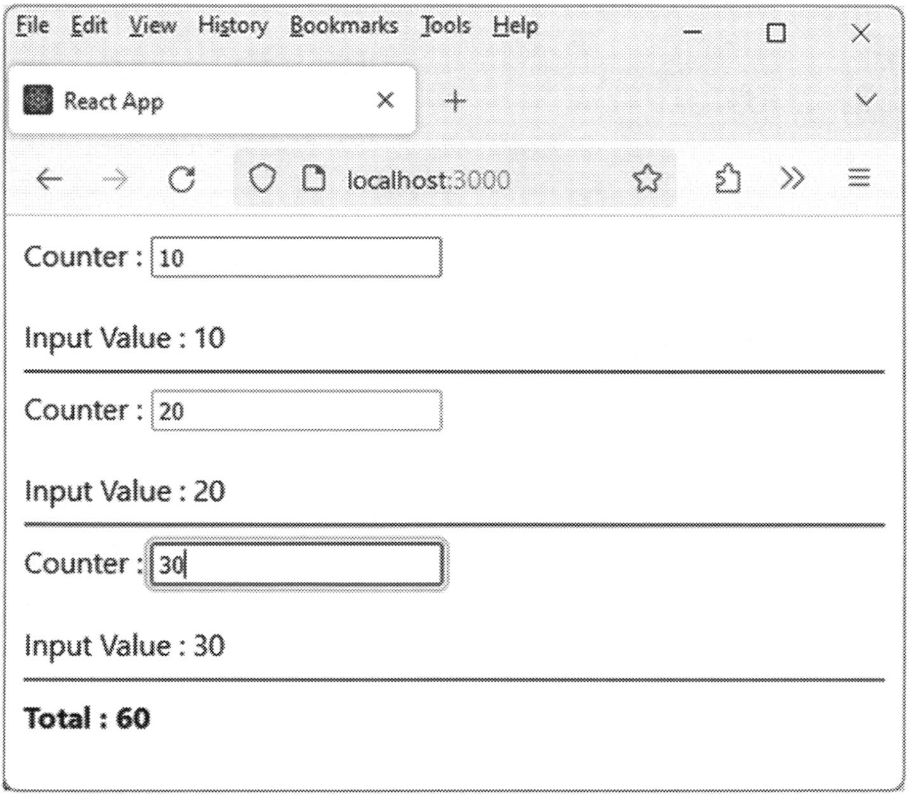

Figure 3-8. *Calculation of the sum of three counters*

To achieve this, we modify the App and Counter components. The App component incorporates a new reactive variable named "total", which will display the total of the three counters. This reactive variable "total" is initialized to 0.

App component displaying the counters and the total sum
(file src/App.js)

```
import { useState } from "react";

import logo from './logo.svg';
import './App.css';
import Counter from "./Counter.js";
import React from "react";
function App() {
  const [total, setTotal] = useState(0);
  return (
    <>
      <Counter setTotal={setTotal} /> <hr />
      <Counter setTotal={setTotal} /> <hr />
      <Counter setTotal={setTotal} /> <hr />
      <b>Total : {total}</b>
    </>
  )
}
```

```
export default App;
```

The "total" variable is placed in the state of the App component and is initialized to 0. The setTotal() function returned by useState() is used to update this reactive variable.

This setTotal() function is passed as an attribute to the Counter component so that it can be used to update the displayed total.

The Counter component, which uses the setTotal() function passed as an attribute, becomes as follows:

Counter component using the setTotal() method defined in the App component (file src/Counter.js)

```
import { useState, useEffect, useRef } from "react";

function Counter({setTotal}) {
  const [value, setValue] = useState("");
  const refCounter = useRef();

  useEffect(function() {
    refCounter.current.focus();   // refCounter.current
    represents the DOM element associated with that reference
  }, []);

  function change(event) {
    var newValue = parseInt(event.target.value||0);

    // New value in the field
    setValue(newValue);

    // New Total
    setTotal((total)=>(total-value));      // Subtract the
                                              old value
    setTotal((total)=>(total+newValue));  // Add the new value
  }

  function keydown(event) {
    // Display the pressed key in the console
    console.log(event.key);
    // Allow the Backspace, Delete, ArrowLeft, ArrowRight, and
      Tab keys
```

```
  if (["Backspace", "Delete", "ArrowLeft", "ArrowRight",
  "Tab"].includes(event.key)) return;
  // Then disallow all other keys except those from 0 to 9
  if (event.key < "0" || event.key > "9") event.
  preventDefault();
}

return (
  <>
    Counter : <input type="text" onChange={change}
    onKeyDown={keydown} ref={refCounter} /> <br/><br/>
    Input Value : {value}
  </>
)
}

export default Counter;
```

The calculation of the new total is performed as follows:

- We subtract the old value of the field from the total.

- Then we add the new value of the field to the total.

For example, if we type 30 in the last counter, when entering the 0, we subtract the value 3 from the total and then add the value 30.

Notice that we pass the setTotal() function to the Counter component, but we don't pass the "total" variable. It's not necessary to pass the "total" variable because we use the setTotal(callback) function, using the callback function as a parameter to update the total (the total is passed as a parameter in the callback function).

Now, let's see how to further improve the functionality of this program.

Step 4: Give Focus to the First Displayed Counter

When you launch the previous program, you might notice that the input field of the last displayed counter is the one that gains focus. This is because the Counter component gives focus to the input field, and thus the last displayed counter obtains focus in the end.

Instead, we want to assign focus to the input field of the Counter component for which a new attribute, let's call it "focus", is indicated. The presence of the "focus" attribute in a Counter component will indicate that this Counter component should have focus:

- If multiple Counter components have this attribute, the last indicated Counter component will receive focus.

- If no Counter component has the "focus" attribute, focus will not be assigned to any field.

Both the App and Counter components are modified. In the App component, we indicate that the first Counter component should receive focus by using the "focus" attribute in that component:

App component indicating the "focus" attribute in a Counter component (file src/App.js)

```
import { useState } from "react";

import logo from './logo.svg';
import './App.css';
import Counter from "./Counter.js";
import React from "react";
function App() {
  const [total, setTotal] = useState(0);
  return (
    <>
```

```
    <Counter focus setTotal={setTotal} /> <hr />
    <Counter setTotal={setTotal} /> <hr />
    <Counter setTotal={setTotal} /> <hr />
    <b>Total : {total}</b>
  </>
)
}
```

```
export default App;
```

So, we indicate the "focus" attribute in the first Counter component. It is not necessary to provide a value for this attribute; its presence alone is sufficient to indicate that this component should have focus.

The Counter component incorporating the "focus" attribute and assigning focus to the component that uses this attribute becomes

Counter component using the "focus" attribute (file src/Counter.js)

```
import { useState, useEffect, useRef } from "react";

function Counter({setTotal, focus}) {
  const [value, setValue] = useState("");
  const refCounter = useRef();

  useEffect(function() {
    // Give focus to the field if the "focus" attribute is
       indicated
    if (focus) refCounter.current.focus();
  }, []);

  function change(event) {
    var newValue = parseInt(event.target.value||0);

    // New value in the field
    setValue(newValue);
```

```
    // New Total
    setTotal((total)=>(total-value));     // Subtract the
                                             old value
    setTotal((total)=>(total+newValue));  // Add the new value
  }

  function keydown(event) {
    // Display the pressed key in the console
    console.log(event.key);
    // Allow the Backspace, Delete, ArrowLeft, ArrowRight, and
       Tab keys
    if (["Backspace", "Delete", "ArrowLeft", "ArrowRight",
    "Tab"].includes(event.key)) return;
    // Then disallow all other keys except those from 0 to 9
    if (event.key < "0" || event.key > "9") event.
    preventDefault();
  }

  return (
    <>
      Counter : <input type="text" onChange={change}
      onKeyDown={keydown} ref={refCounter} /> <br/><br/>
      Input Value : {value}
    </>
  )
}

export default Counter;
```

We verify that the first counter now has the focus (Figure 3-9).

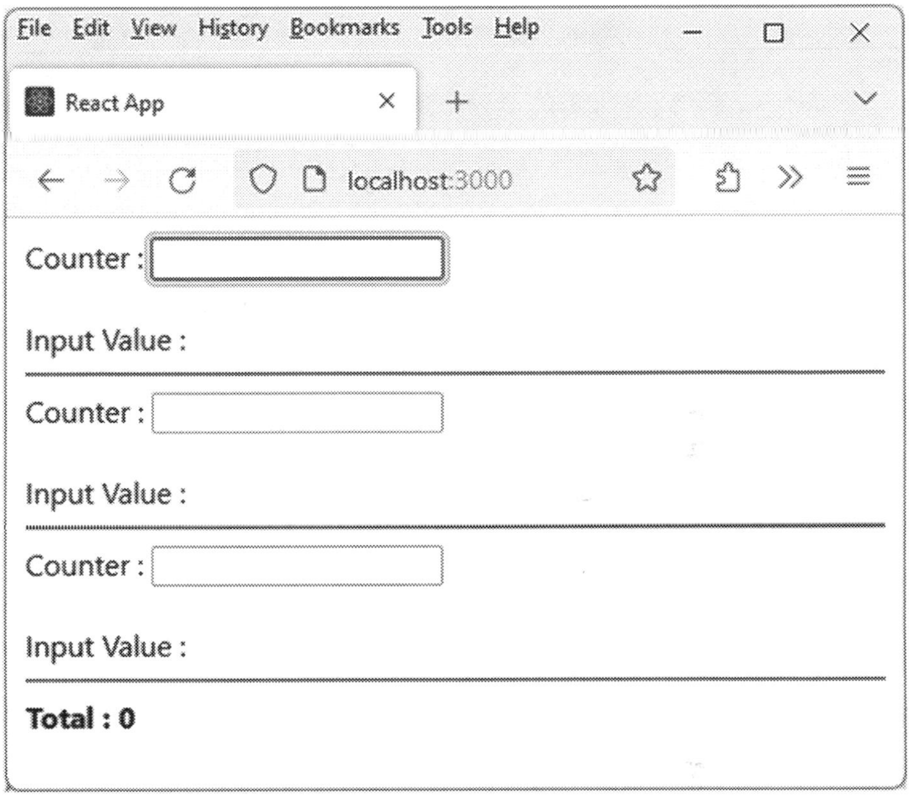

Figure 3-9. *The first displayed counter gains focus*

Conclusion

The third day of our journey into learning React was dedicated to event handling with React. We learned how to create event handlers in our React components to make our user interface more interactive.

We are now prepared to continue our exploration of React and delve deeper into the possibilities offered by this exciting JavaScript library, as we move on to a comprehensive study of React hooks.

CHAPTER 4

Day 4: Mastering React Hooks

In this chapter, we will dive deeper into a feature of React: hooks.

In the previous pages, we covered some hooks, such as useState(), useEffect(), and useRef(). We will now recap this knowledge, dive deeper, and also discover new hooks we haven't used yet.

Hooks are a feature introduced in React 16.8 that allows developers to reuse component logic by separating state and effects logic from display logic. Hooks are functions that allow access to state, effects, and other React features in functional components.

Throughout this chapter, you will learn how to better utilize hooks in your components, how to create custom hooks, and how to reuse logic in your React applications.

Are you ready to dive into React hooks? Let's get started!

Definition of a Hook

React hooks, introduced in recent versions of React (starting from version 16.8), have simplified the design and programming of React components. They have notably brought reactivity to components defined as JavaScript functions, which previously was only possible with components described as JavaScript classes. This has greatly simplified component programming with React.

© Eric Sarrion 2023
E. Sarrion, *Master React in 5 Days*, https://doi.org/10.1007/978-1-4842-9855-8_4

In general, a hook corresponds to a method defined in React. To use a hook in a component, you need to import the corresponding method using the JavaScript import statement.

Hooks defined by React all start with the word use, followed by the name of the hook you want to use. For example, useState is used to manage state, that is, reactive variables, while useEffect is used for managing effects. You can also define your own custom hooks and use them like those defined by React.

Main Rule About Hooks

The main rule about hooks can be summarized in the following two points:

- Hooks must be used sequentially.

- Hooks must be used only in functions that define React components.

Using hooks sequentially means that they cannot be used, for example, within a condition or a loop. The use instructions associated with hooks must be used directly in the function that defines the component, at the top level of the function.

Regardless of the conditions of use for the component that uses one or more hooks, the order of hook calls inside the component must always be the same and should not be used, for example, within a condition.

React has defined a number of standard hooks for common use cases. For example,

- The useState() method is used to define a reactive variable. Modifying the variable in the program will automatically update it (thanks to React) wherever the variable is used in the displayed page.

- The useRef() method is used to define a nonreactive variable. Modifying the variable in the program will not affect its displayed value on the page (as long as the component is not updated due to a modification of one of its reactive variables)

- The useEffect() method is used to define blocks of code that will be executed when the component is created or updated under certain conditions.

- The useReducer() method is used to manage a reactive variable based on actions defined in the program. It offers more possibilities than the previous useState() method.

Let's see in the following sections how to use each of these methods. Note that we have already used and explained some of these methods in the previous pages of this book. The goal here is to centralize the explanations to provide a better understanding of how these methods work.

Using the useState( ) Hook

The useState(initValue) method is used to create a reactive variable. A variable is considered reactive if its internal modification (within the program) changes the displayed value in the HTML page wherever that variable is used. React internally uses a process to update the DOM whenever a reactive variable is modified.

The useState(initValue) method can be used to create as many reactive variables as desired. These variables will be local to the component in which they are created. The initValue parameter corresponds to the initial value of the variable. If not specified, the initial value is undefined.

Step 1: Writing the useState() Method

The useState() method returns an array containing two values:

- The first value of the returned array (at index 0) corresponds to the value of the reactive variable.

- The second value of the returned array (at index 1) is a function used to update the value of this reactive variable. Indeed, a reactive variable is not updated directly by assigning it a new value; you should exclusively use the update function returned by the useState() method.

It is common to use array destructuring, a feature allowed by recent versions of JavaScript, which can be written as follows:

Using destructuring to retrieve the result of useState()

```
const [value, setValue] = useState();
```

The variable value corresponds to the value of the reactive variable, while setValue is the function that allows updating this variable using setValue(newValue).

Let's write a Counter component that increments a variable value upon clicking a button. The variable value represents the counter value and is displayed next to the button.

Counter component for incrementing a variable (file src/Counter.js)

```
import { useState } from "react";

function Counter() {
  const [value, setValue] = useState(0);

  function incrValue() {
    setValue(value+1);
```

```
    }
    return (
      <>
        <button onClick={incrValue}>value + 1</button>
         =>
        value = {value};
          
      </>
    )
}

export default Counter;
```

We have described the Counter component here. It utilizes the reactive variable value which will be incremented upon clicking the button.

The Counter component is then used within the App component. We place it in two locations within the App component, thus displaying two counters. This demonstrates that each Counter component has its own independent reactive variables (separate from other components).

App component using the Counter component (file src/App.js)

```
import logo from './logo.svg';
import './App.css';
import Counter from "./Counter.js";
import React from "react";
function App() {
  return (
    <>
      Counter#1 : <Counter />
      <hr style={{margin:'10px', height:'3px',
      backgroundColor:'gray'}}/>
```

```
      Counter#2 : <Counter />
    </>
  )
}
```

```
export default App;
```

A horizontal rule <hr> separates the two displayed Counter components (Figure 4-1).

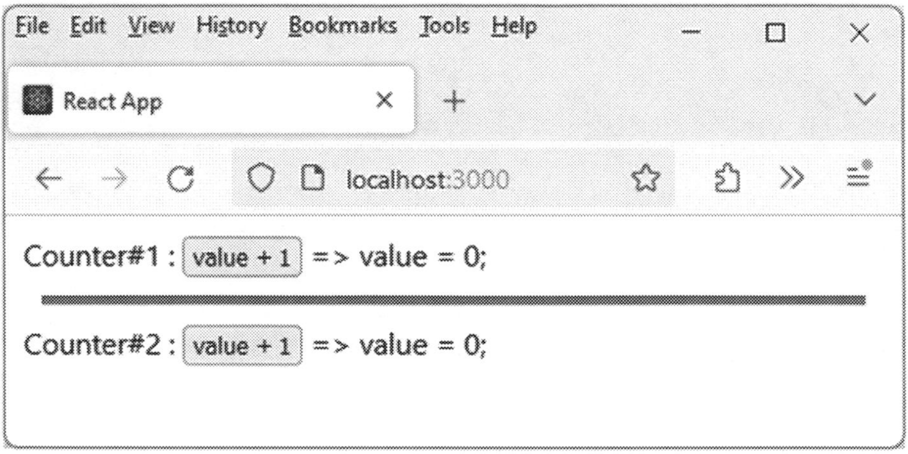

Figure 4-1. *Counters incremented by clicking a button*

Let's click twice on the first button and three times on the second (Figure 4-2).

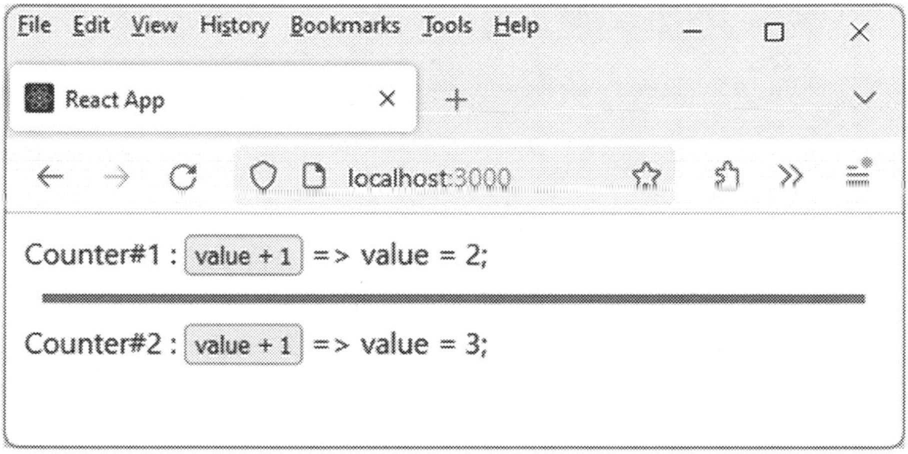

Figure 4-2. *Counters incrementation*

This shows that each reactive variable "value" is independent within each component.

Step 2: Using the Latest Value of the Reactive Variable

There are cases where a reactive variable is modified in the program, but its new value is not immediately assigned. For example, if we increment the counter twice in a row with each button click, only the first increment is considered:

Counter component that increments a variable only once (file src/Counter.js)

```
import { useState, useEffect } from "react";

function Counter() {
  const [value, setValue] = useState(0);
```

```
function incrValue() {
  setValue(value+1);    // The value of "value" is modified,
  setValue(value+1);    // but here we are using the old
                        value of "value"
                        // (not the one that has just been
                        incremented).
}

return (
  <>
    <button onClick={incrValue}>value + 1</button>
     =>
    value = {value};
  </>
)
}

export default Counter;
```

Each button click increases "value" by 1 instead of 2 as expected
(Figure 4-3).

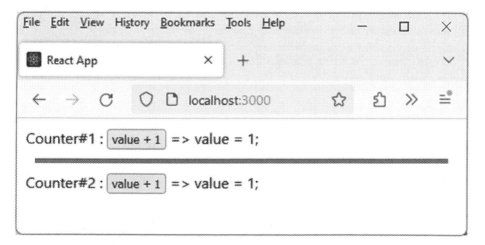

Figure 4-3. *Incrementing by 1 instead of 2*

In this program, when the incrValue() function is called, it updates the value of "value" twice in a row by calling the setValue() function twice. However, each call to setValue() triggers a new component render, but the value update isn't immediate.

Instead, React schedules the value update for the next render, due to how state updates are handled asynchronously. As a result, when setValue(value+1) is called twice in a row, the value of "value" is actually updated only once.

Reconciliation Process:

When a reactive variable is defined with useState() and modified in the program, the modification isn't immediately visible because React uses a process called "reconciliation." This means React compares the new state of the variable with its previous state and determines what has changed. Then, React updates the DOM to reflect those changes.

This reconciliation process is what makes React highly performant, as it updates only the parts of the DOM that need to be updated, rather than reloading the entire page. However, it also means that updates are not instantaneous. This can sometimes lead to issues if parts of the code depend on the current state of the variable before reconciliation is done.

In other words, the second call to setValue() uses the initial value of "value" instead of the value that has just been updated. This means the final value of "value" will only increment by 1 with each click, even if there are two successive calls to setValue().

To avoid this issue, you should use the version of the update function setValue(callback) that takes a callback function as a parameter. The callback function in the form callback(value) will then use the latest value of the "value" variable as a parameter.

Counter component using setValue(callback) (file src/Counter.js)

```
import { useState } from "react";

function Counter() {
```

```
const [value, setValue] = useState(0);

function incrValue() {
  // setValue(value+1);
  // setValue(value+1);
  setValue(function(value) { return value+1 });    // "value"
  is updated,
  setValue(function(value) { return value+1 });    // then we
  use its new value.
}

return (
  <>
    <button onClick={incrValue}>value + 1</button>
     =>
    value = {value};
  </>
)
}

export default Counter;
```

It is especially the second increment of the variable using setValue() that requires using it in the form of setValue(callback).

With each button click, the value is now incremented twice (Figure 4-4).

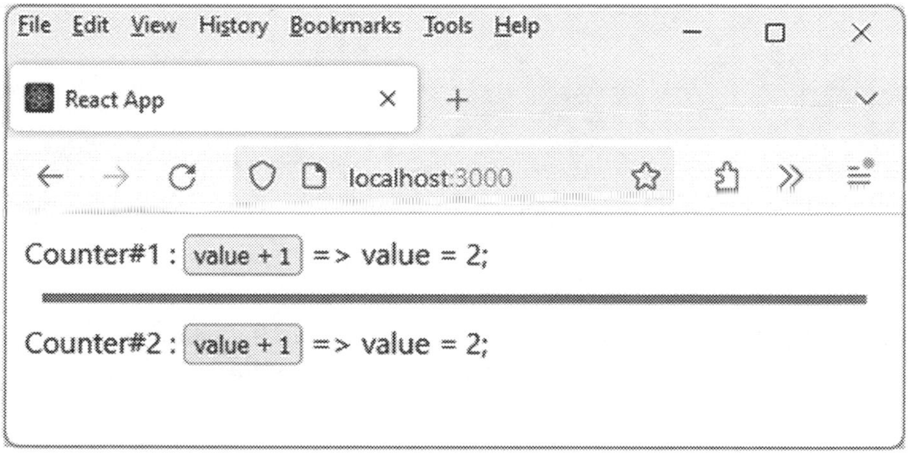

Figure 4-4. *Increment of 2 instead of 1*

Step 3: Avoiding Infinite Loops When Updating Reactive Variables

When a reactive variable is updated, it triggers an update of the displayed component during the reconciliation process, leading to the execution of the associated component function. However, if a reactive variable is updated during this display, it triggers another update of the display, potentially causing an endless loop.

This can be observed in the following program, which updates the reactive variable "value" during the component display:

Counter component with infinite loop (file src/Counter.js)

```
import { useState } from "react";

function Counter() {
  const [value, setValue] = useState(0);
```

```
function incrValue() {
  setValue(value+1);
}

setValue(1);

return (
  <>
    <button onClick={incrValue}>value + 1</button>
     =>
    value = {value};
  </>
)
}
```

```
export default Counter;
```

The previous program triggers an infinite loop because setValue(1) is called each time the component is rendered. This sets off a chain reaction where the component is constantly updated, leading to an endless rendering loop.

The incrValue() function, triggered when clicking the button, also calls setValue(), but it doesn't cause an infinite loop because setValue(value+1) is asynchronously invoked (only upon button click) and doesn't immediately update the value of "value".

On the other hand, the line setValue(1) outside the incrValue() function is synchronously executed every time the component is rendered, causing the value update to be constantly triggered, creating an infinite loop.

As a result, the Counter component cannot be displayed in the window, and an error message is shown in Figure 4-5 (including in the console).

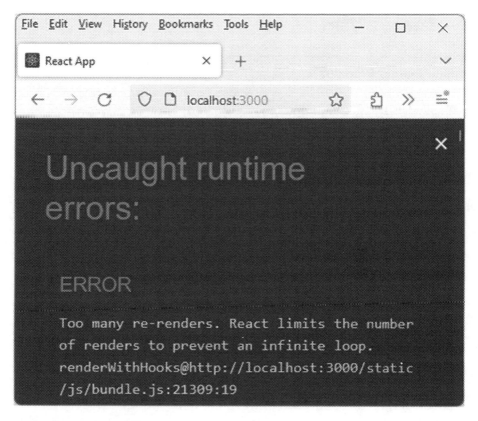

Figure 4-5. *Error "Too many re-renders"*

To solve the infinite loop problem in the program using useState(), you can use the useEffect() hook to execute the reactive variable update code under certain conditions. This can be achieved by passing the "conditions" parameter in the dependency array of useEffect(callback, conditions).

Counter component using the useEffect() hook (file src/Counter.js)

```
import { useState, useEffect } from "react";

function Counter() {
  const [value, setValue] = useState(0);

  function incrValue() {
```

121

```
  setValue(value+1);
}

useEffect(function() {
  setValue(1);
}, []);  // conditions = [] means that setValue(1) is
        executed only on the initial display.

return (
  <>
    <button onClick={incrValue}>value + 1</button>
     =>
    value = {value};
  </>
)
}

export default Counter;
```

The instruction setValue(1) is now executed only once, during the initial display of the component (after it has been rendered). This is because of the "conditions" parameter of the useEffect() method initialized as [], which means to execute the hook's processing only after the initial component rendering. We can see in Figure 4-6 that the error has disapeared.

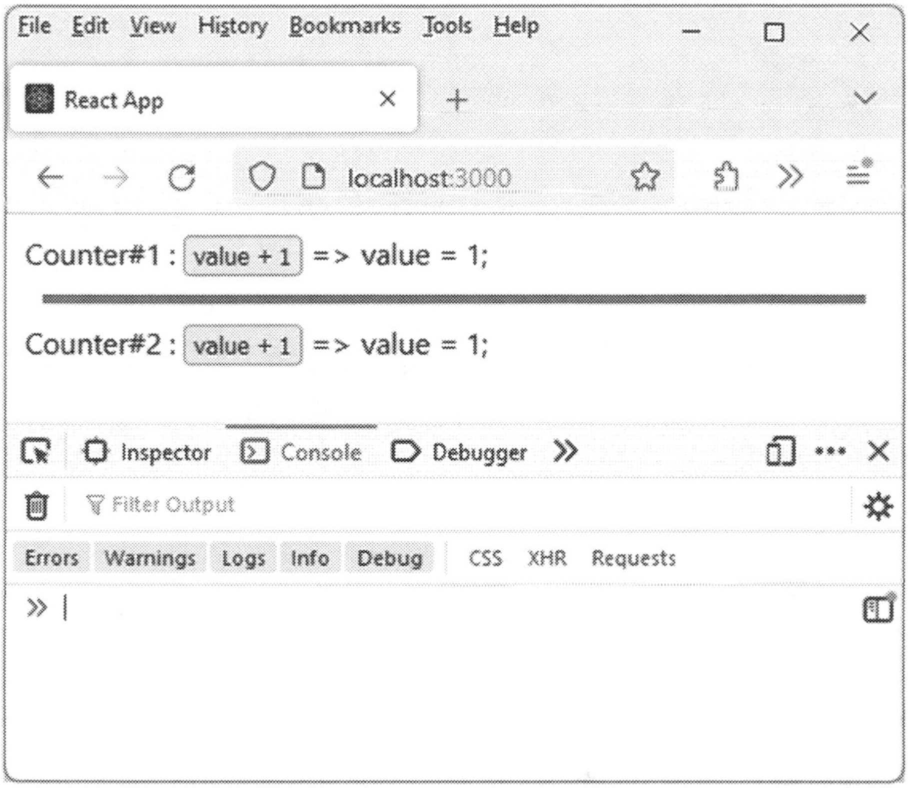

Figure 4-6. *The "value" variable is directly set to 1*

We can observe that there are no more error messages, either on the screen or in the console, and therefore no more infinite loop. This is achieved thanks to the use of the useEffect() hook.

Using the useContext( ) Hook

The useContext() method allows us to define elements (variables, objects, functions) that can be passed and used in internal components.

To better understand the benefit of this hook, let's consider a scenario where we want to display the sum of the previous two counters. We will approach this in two different ways: first, without using the useContext()

hook and then by using it. But let's begin by explaining the problem we want to solve. Once the problem is explained, we will proceed to solve it with or without the useContext() hook.

Step 1: Presenting the Problem to Solve

We want to display the sum of the two counters. Each counter can be incremented by clicking the associated button. Clicking the button not only increments the counter's value but also needs to increment the total sum of the counters, displayed at the bottom of the page.

The sum of the reactive variables defined in each Counter component will be displayed in the App component using a new reactive variable named "total", which will be updated with each button click.

The App component that displays the total values of the counters becomes as follows:

App component displaying the total values of the counters (file src/App.js)

```
import { useState } from "react";
import logo from './logo.svg';
import './App.css';
import Counter from "./Counter.js";
import React from "react";

function App() {
  const [total, setTotal] = useState(0);

  return (
    <>
      Counter#1 : <Counter />
      <hr style={{margin:'10px', height:'3px', background
      Color:'gray'}}/>
      Counter#2 : <Counter />
```

```
    <hr style={{margin:'10px', height:'3px',
    backgroundColor:'gray'}}/>
    <b>Total value = {total}</b>
  </>
  )
}

export default App;
```

The "total" variable is managed by useState(), which also returns the setTotal() method for updating the reactive variable "total".

The Counter component is the same as before. It is reproduced here to show the modifications that will be applied to it later.

Counter component managing the counter increment (file src/ Counter.js)

```
import { useState } from "react";

function Counter() {
  const [value, setValue] = useState(0);

  function incrValue() {
    setValue(value+1);
  }

  return (
    <>
      <button onClick={incrValue}>value + 1</button>
       =>
      value = {value};
        
    </>
  )
}

export default Counter;
```

125

We then obtain the display in Figure 4-7. You will notice that the total of the counters (at the bottom of the page) is not being updated after clicking the buttons.

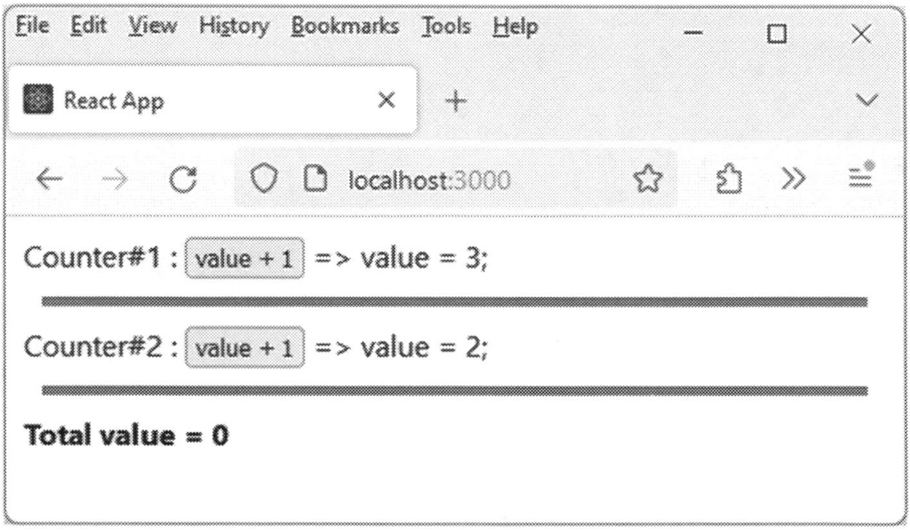

Figure 4-7. *The total of the counters is not being updated*

The total of the counters is not being updated. Indeed, we are using a reactive variable "total" (initialized to 0) that should be incremented with each click on the Counter component's button. For this purpose, the setTotal() method returned by useState() must be used within the Counter component, as it is the only way to update the reactive variable "total".

Updating a reactive variable can only be done using the specialized function returned by useState(), at index 1 of the array returned by useState().

The problem is that the Counter component is not aware of the setTotal() method, as it belongs to the parent App component. We will explore how to allow the Counter component to access the setTotal() method using the useContext() hook or without using it.

Let's start by explaining how to proceed in the case where the useContext() hook is not used.

Step 2: Displaying the Sum of Counters Without Using the useContext( ) Hook

The problem to solve is to enable the Counter component to know about the setTotal() method (which is defined in the parent App component) so that the Counter component can use it when the button "value + 1" is clicked to increment the counter's value.

If we are not using the useContext() hook, the only way to enable the Counter component to access the setTotal() method defined in the parent App component is to pass this method as an attribute to the Counter component when creating it within the App component.

We use an attribute named setTotal (or any other name, but setTotal is easier to remember for later use) in the Counter component. This attribute setTotal will be initialized to a value that is a reference to the setTotal() function. Therefore, we use the Counter component in the form <Counter setTotal={setTotal} />. The setTotal attribute will now be part of the attributes of the Counter component.

The App component is modified to pass the setTotal attribute to the Counter component:

App component using the setTotal attribute when using the Counter component (file src/App.js)

```
import { useState } from "react";
import logo from './logo.svg';
import './App.css';
import Counter from "./Counter.js";
import React from "react";

function App() {
  const [total, setTotal] = useState(0);
```

```
  return (
    <>
      Counter#1 : <Counter setTotal={setTotal} />
      <hr style={{margin:'10px', height:'3px',
      backgroundColor:'gray'}}/>
      Counter#2 : <Counter setTotal={setTotal} />
      <hr style={{margin:'10px', height:'3px',
      backgroundColor:'gray'}}/>
      <b>Total value = {total}</b>
    </>
  )
}

export default App;
```

The setTotal attribute is placed wherever the Counter component is used, which includes when writing the two Counter components.

Then, the Counter component is also modified to consider the setTotal attribute and use it to increment the total of the counters:

Counter component using the setTotal attribute (file src/Counter.js)

```
import { useState } from "react";

function Counter({setTotal}) {
  const [value, setValue] = useState(0);

  function incrValue() {
    setValue(value+1);
    setTotal((total)=>total+1);
  }

  return (
```

```
    <>
      <button onClick={incrValue}>value + 1</button>
       =>
      value = {value};
        
    </>
  )
}

export default Counter;
```

Note that the setTotal() function uses the setTotal(callback) form, in which the callback function has the "total" parameter, which represents the current value of the reactive variable "total". Indeed, there is no other way to know the value of the "total" variable than to use this form of the setTotal(callback) method; otherwise, the "total" variable would be inaccessible (outside of the callback function).

Let's verify that the total of the counters is now displayed correctly (see Figure 4-8).

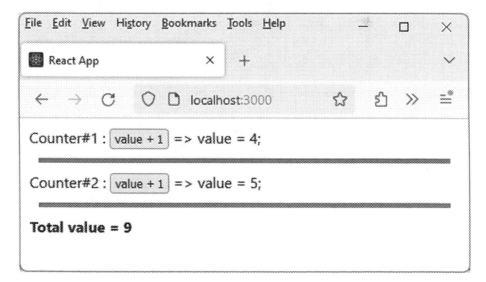

Figure 4-8. *The total of the counters is displayed correctly*

We have seen the first way of passing data to a child component, using attributes. Let's now explore the second way, which is to use the useContext() hook provided by React.

Step 3: Displaying the Sum of Counters Using the useContext() Hook

Instead of passing the setTotal() function as an attribute to the Counter component, we make this function available to all components that are descendants. This means that from the App component, we make the setTotal() function available to child components, here, available in the Counter components used within the parent App component.

To achieve this, React provides us with the createContext() and useContext() methods:

- The createContext() method is used in the parent component that makes certain functionalities available.

- The useContext() method is used in child components to use the functionalities made available.

Let's now see how to use each of these two methods, starting with the createContext() method.

Step 4: Using the createContext() Method in the Parent Component

Let's first see how to use the createContext() method in the parent App component.

Using the createContext() method in the App component (file src/App.js)

```
import { useState, createContext } from "react";
import logo from './logo.svg';
import './App.css';
import Counter from "./Counter.js";
import React from "react";

const TotalContext = createContext();

function App() {
  const [total, setTotal] = useState(0);

  return (
    <>
      <TotalContext.Provider value={[total, setTotal]}>
        Counter#1 : <Counter />
        <hr style={{margin:'10px', height:'3px',
        backgroundColor:'gray'}}/>
        Counter#2 : <Counter />
        <hr style={{margin:'10px', height:'3px',
        backgroundColor:'gray'}}/>
        <b>Total value = {total}</b>
      </TotalContext.Provider>
    </>
  )
}

// export default App;
export { App, TotalContext };
```

The createContext() method is first imported from the "react" module. Next, we create a context (here named TotalContext) using the createContext() method. This provides us with the new TotalContext. Provider component, whose value attribute indicates the resources made available to child components.

In this case, we want to make the reactive variable "total" and its setTotal() update function available. To provide other information, you can simply include them in the array placed in the value attribute of the TotalContext.Provider component.

Furthermore, we want the TotalContext context to be accessible in child components, including the Counter component. To achieve this, we need to export this element. Therefore, we replace the export default App statement with export { App, TotalContext } to make both the App and TotalContext objects available.

If you use export { App, TotalContext } instead of export default App in the App.js file, you also need to modify the index.js file, which imports the App component. Replace the import App from './App'; statement with import { App } from './App';.

This results in the following modified index.js file:

Modifying the index.js file (file src/index.js)

```
import React from 'react';
import ReactDOM from 'react-dom/client';
import './index.css';
// import App from './App';
import { App } from './App';
import reportWebVitals from './reportWebVitals';

const root = ReactDOM.createRoot(document.
getElementById('root'));
root.render(
  <App />
);

// If you want to start measuring performance in your app, pass
a function
// to log results (for example: reportWebVitals(console.log))
```

```
// or send to an analytics endpoint. Learn more: https://bit.
ly/CRA-vitals
reportWebVitals();
```

The desired elements have now been made available in the parent component, and the next step is to use them in the child components. Let's see how to do that.

Step 5: Using the useContext( ) Method in Child Components

Once the elements are made available in the parent component, the next step is to use them in the child components. To do this, we use the useContext() hook in the child Counter component. The setTotal() function made available will thus be accessible in the Counter component.

Using the useContext() method in the Counter component (file src/ Counter.js)

```
import { useState, useContext } from "react";
import { TotalContext } from "./App";

function Counter() {
  const [value, setValue] = useState(0);
  const [total, setTotal] = useContext(TotalContext);

  function incrValue() {
    setValue(value+1);
    setTotal((total)=>total+1);
  }

  return (
    <>
      <button onClick={incrValue}>value + 1</button>
       =>
```

```
      value = {value};
        
    </>
  )
}
```

```
export default Counter;
```

The useContext() hook is imported from the "react" module, while the TotalContext context is imported from the App component.

The useContext(TotalContext) method allows us to retrieve the value of the value attribute set in the TotalContext.Provider component. This way, we retrieve the array [total, setTotal], which allows us to use the setTotal() function that modifies the reactive variable "total".

Let's verify that the functionality is correct (see Figure 4-9).

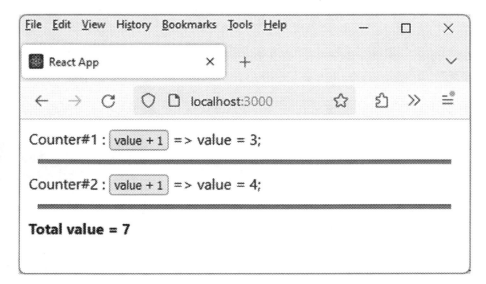

Figure 4-9. *The total is incremented correctly*

Step 6: When to Use the useContext( ) Hook?

As seen earlier, using the useContext() hook requires some preparation in different files to set it up. This approach can be beneficial if multiple components need access to higher-level reactive variables, or if many reactive variables need to be shared with various components.

However, if you only need to provide access to a few reactive variables or components, you might prefer the first solution, which is to pass the reactive variable update function in the attributes of the components that will use it.

Using the useRef( ) Hook

The useRef() hook is used in two distinct cases:

- It is used if you want to access specific DOM elements defined in the JSX code of the component. In this case, you will use the ref attribute when writing this element in the JSX code, and the correspondence with the value returned by the useRef() hook will be established in a useEffect() method. We saw this case in the previous chapter when we wanted to give focus to an input field.

- It is also used if you want to create nonreactive variables, which can be updated without causing the component to re-render.

The first use case of useRef() has already been explained earlier. Let's now examine the second use case in detail.

The useRef(initValue) hook allows you to create nonreactive variables, meaning that updating them will not trigger a re-render of the containing component. This functionality enables you to update variables (created using useRef()) in a component without causing it to re-render:

- Updating a reactive variable created using useState() triggers a re-render of the component in which it is created.

- Conversely, updating a nonreactive variable created using useRef() does not trigger a re-render of the component in which it is created.

Let's demonstrate how to use useRef() to maintain information without using a reactive variable.

We will use the Counter component, which now displays two buttons for incrementing two types of variables:

- The "value + 1" button increments the reactive variable "value" created using useState(), as seen previously, and displays it next to the button.

- The "ref + 1" button increments the "ref" variable created using useRef(). The value of this "ref" variable is displayed next to the button.

The Counter component's file is modified to handle these two types of variables. This allows us to visualize the difference in behavior between reactive and nonreactive variables.

Updating variables defined using useState() and useRef()
(file src/Counter.js)

```
import { useState, useRef } from "react";

function Counter() {
```

```
  const [value, setValue] = useState(0);
  const valueRef = useRef(0);

  function incrValue() {
    setValue(value+1);
  }

  function incrRef() {
    valueRef.current += 1;
  }

  return (
    <>
      <button onClick={incrValue}>value + 1</button>
       =>
      value = {value};
        

      <button onClick={incrRef}>ref + 1</button>
       =>
      ref = {valueRef.current};
        
    </>
  )
}

export default Counter;
```

The value of the variable created using useRef() is obtained through the "current" property of the object returned by useRef(). The variable is initialized to the value specified in the initValue parameter, or to undefined if no value is provided in this parameter.

The file of the App component is restored to its original content, which displays the two Counter components separated by a horizontal line.

App component displaying the two Counter components (file src/App.js)

```
import logo from './logo.svg';
import './App.css';
import Counter from "./Counter.js";

function App() {
  return (
    <>
      Counter#1 : <Counter />
      <hr style={{margin:'10px', height:'3px',
      backgroundColor:'gray'}}/>
      Counter#2 : <Counter />
    </>
  )
}

export default App;
```

Also, the index.js file is restored to its previous version:

File src/index.js

```
import React from 'react';
import ReactDOM from 'react-dom/client';
import './index.css';
import App from './App';
import reportWebVitals from './reportWebVitals';

const root = ReactDOM.createRoot(document.
getElementById('root'));
root.render(
  <App />
);
```

```
// If you want to start measuring performance in your app, pass
a function
// to log results (for example: reportWebVitals(console.log))
// or send to an analytics endpoint. Learn more: https://bit.
ly/CRA-vitals
reportWebVitals();
```

The display in Figure 4-10 is obtained.

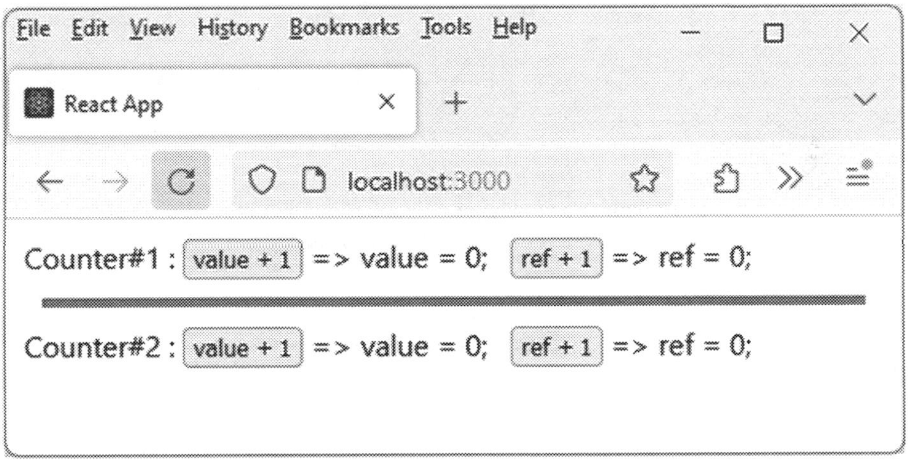

Figure 4-10. *Using a variable with useRef()*

The "value + 1" button increments the reactive variable "value", while the "ref + 1" button increments the nonreactive variable "ref".

Let's click once each "value + 1" button: the reactive variable "value" displayed next to each button increments upon clicking, which is an expected behavior since updating a reactive variable refreshes the component in which it is used (Figure 4-11).

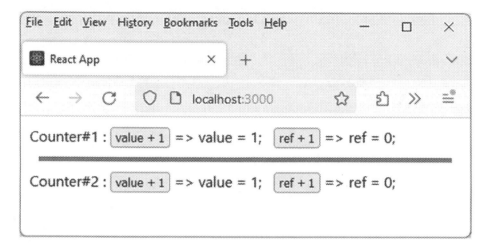

Figure 4-11. *Incrementing the reactive variable "value"*

Now let's click once each "ref + 1" button (Figure 4-12).

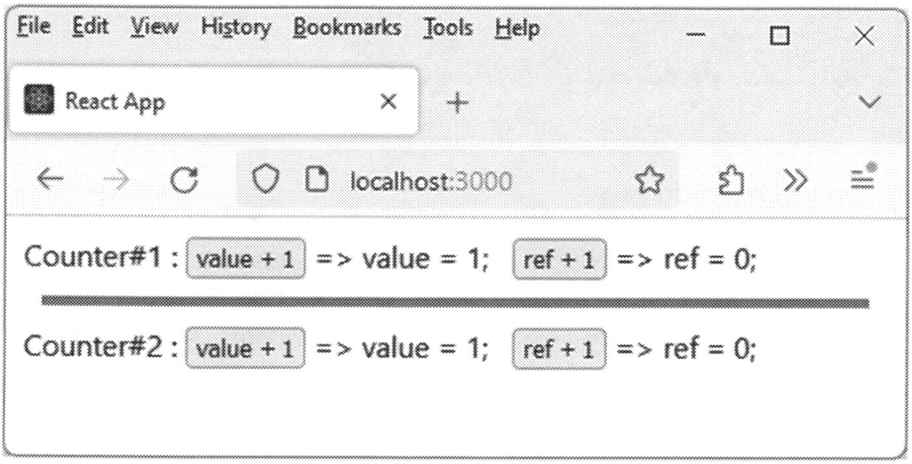

Figure 4-12. *Incrementing the nonreactive variable "ref"*

We observe that the increment of the nonreactive variable "ref" is not visible on the screen. While the "ref" variable is incremented, since it is not reactive (meaning it doesn't trigger a re-render of the containing displayed component), its displayed value remains unchanged. To view the updated value of the "ref" variable, you simply need to refresh the component that contains it. To do this, let's click once the first "value + 1" button (Figure 4-13). This action, which updates the reactive variable "value" of the first displayed Counter component, also triggers the display of the new value of the nonreactive "ref" variable within the refreshed component

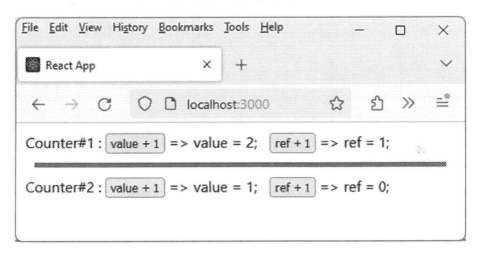

Figure 4-13. *Refreshing the first Counter component*

We can see that the displayed "ref" variable in the first component has been refreshed, as updating a reactive variable triggers an update of the containing component. Additionally, the "value" variable of this component, being reactive, has also incremented due to the click.

To trigger the update of the "ref" variable in the second Counter component, it is sufficient to update the reactive "value" variable associated with that component. Let's click the second "value + 1" button (Figure 4-14).

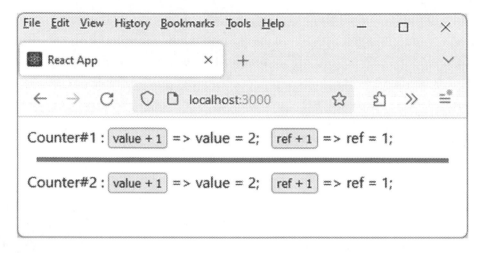

Figure 4-14. *Refreshing the second Counter component*

The "ref" variable of the second Counter component has now been updated. The useRef() hook is ideal for storing persistent values without triggering re-renders, providing an alternative to useState(). This makes it perfect for DOM elements, counters, and temporary values. Therefore, useState() is used to manage state affecting display, while useRef() is used for persistence without disrupting the user interface.

Using the useEffect( ) Hook

The useEffect(callback, dependencies) method used within a component allows you to group a set of instructions that will be executed under certain conditions. The instructions to be executed are expressed within the callback function, while the conditions are specified by the dependencies parameter.

It's possible to use the useEffect() method multiple times in a component, with different instructions specified in each callback function, or different dependencies for each of them. During the initial render of the component, the callback function is always executed regardless of the conditions specified. During subsequent updates of the component, the callback function is executed based on the conditions expressed in the dependencies parameter.

Remember that an update to a component occurs if any of its reactive variables are modified. In all cases, the callback functions registered in the useEffect() methods are executed after the component has been displayed or updated.

The dependencies parameter is the second parameter of the useEffect(callback, dependencies) method. It is used when component updates occur. It corresponds to an array that can have three types of values, indicating whether or not to execute the callback function specified as the first parameter:

> If the dependencies parameter is not specified (or is null or undefined), the callback function specified in useEffect(callback, dependencies) is executed for the initial render and for each subsequent update of the component.

> If the dependencies parameter is an empty array, the callback function specified in useEffect(callback, dependencies) will be executed only during the initial render of the component. If the component is updated, the callback function will not be executed.

> If the dependencies parameter is a non-empty array [value1, value2, ...], the callback function specified in useEffect(callback, dependencies) will be executed for the initial render of the component and then for subsequent updates if at least one of the values valueX in the array has changed since the last execution of the callback function.

Furthermore, each callback function can return a cleanup function that will be executed before the component is updated. This allows for preparation of the following update (e.g., stopping a timer before restarting it later).

To better visualize and understand these explanations, here is a program that uses the previous Counter component. We utilize three useEffect() methods in the program, each using one of the three types of conditions mentioned earlier:

- The first useEffect() method doesn't use any conditions. Therefore, it will be executed during the initial render and with each subsequent update of the component.

- The second useEffect() method uses an empty array as conditions. Thus, it will be executed only during the initial render of the component.

- The third useEffect() method uses an array containing valueRef.current as conditions. As a result, it will be executed during the initial render and with each subsequent update of the component, only if this value has changed since the previous execution. Recall that this value is modified by clicking the "ref + 1" button.

Each of the callback functions associated with the aforementioned useEffect() methods displays a message in the console to indicate which counter it is using, which useEffect() method it pertains to, and the values of the variables value and valueRef. In each of the useEffect() methods, we return a cleanup function. Recall that a function returned by useEffect() will be called before the next update of the component. We will display similar console messages as before, to demonstrate the execution of this function.

The App and Counter components are modified to achieve this. Let's start by describing the App component. It uses a new attribute called "name" in the Counter component, allowing each counter to be named. This helps identify which counter is performing its display or update. It is used as follows:

App component that uses the "name" attribute for the Counter
component (file src/App.js)

```
import logo from './logo.svg';
import './App.css';
import Counter from "./Counter.js";

function App() {
  return (
    <>
      Counter#1 : <Counter name="Counter#1" />
      <hr style={{margin:'10px', height:'3px',
      backgroundColor:'gray'}}/>
      Counter#2 : <Counter name="Counter#2" />
    </>
  )
}

export default App;
```

Here is now the Counter component containing the various uses of
useEffect() described earlier:

Counter component using useEffect() (file src/Counter.js)

```
import { useState, useEffect, useRef } from "react";

function Counter({name}) {
  const [value, setValue] = useState(0);
  const valueRef = useRef(0);

  function incrValue() {
    setValue(value+1);
  }

  function incrRef() {
    valueRef.current += 1;
  }
```

```javascript
  // useEffect#1: used without conditions
  useEffect(function() {
    console.log(
      `${name} useEffect#1: value = ${value}, valueRef.current
      = ${valueRef.current}`
    );
    return function() {
      console.log(
        `${name} return useEffect#1: value = ${value},
        valueRef.current = ${valueRef.current}`
      );
    };
  });

  // useEffect#2: used with conditions = []
  useEffect(function() {
    console.log(
      `${name} useEffect#2: value = ${value}, valueRef.current
      = ${valueRef.current}`
    );
    return function() {
      console.log(
        `${name} return useEffect#2: value = ${value},
        valueRef.current = ${valueRef.current}`
      );
    };
  }, []);

  // useEffect#3: used with conditions = [valueRef.current]
  useEffect(function() {
    console.log(
```

```
      `${name} useEffect#3: value = ${value}, valueRef.current
      = ${valueRef.current}`
    );
    return function() {
      console.log(
        `${name} return useEffect#3: value = ${value},
        valueRef.current = ${valueRef.current}`
      );
    };
  }, [valueRef.current]);

  console.log(`${name} Outside of useEffect()`);

  return (
    <>
      <button onClick={incrValue}>value + 1</button>
       =>
      value = {value};
        

      <button onClick={incrRef}>ref + 1</button>
       =>
      ref = {valueRef.current};
        
    </>
  )
}

export default Counter;
```

In addition to the logs used within the useEffect() methods, we display a log outside of the useEffect() methods. This allows us to verify that the code inside the useEffect() methods is executed after the component is displayed or updated.

We also use a new attribute in the Counter component, which is the "name" attribute, passed from the App component. This attribute will display the name of the Counter component that shows the message in the console logs.

Let's observe the messages displayed in the console based on the button clicks.

Upon launching the program, we have the display in Figure 4-15.

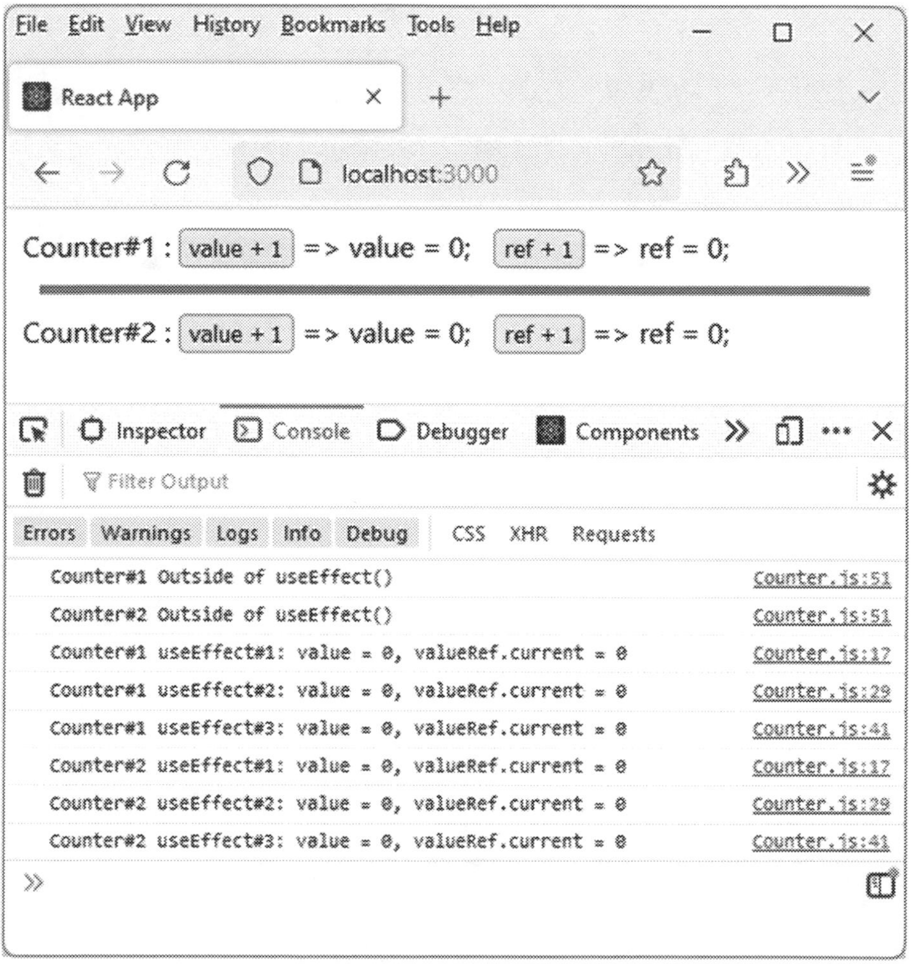

Figure 4-15. At program launch

Upon launching the program corresponding to the initial display of components, the code outside of any effects is executed first, and then the effects are executed in the order they are written in the component (for each of the components).

In order to clearly view the upcoming console messages, let's clear the currently displayed messages (by clicking the associated trash button).

Next, we click the "ref + 1" button associated with the first counter. No message is displayed in the console, and no changes appear on the screen. This is normal because the component is not refreshed since no reactive variable has been updated.

Then, let's click the "value + 1" button associated with the first counter. Since the "value" variable is reactive, the first component is refreshed, and the useEffect() methods are executed (Figure 4-16).

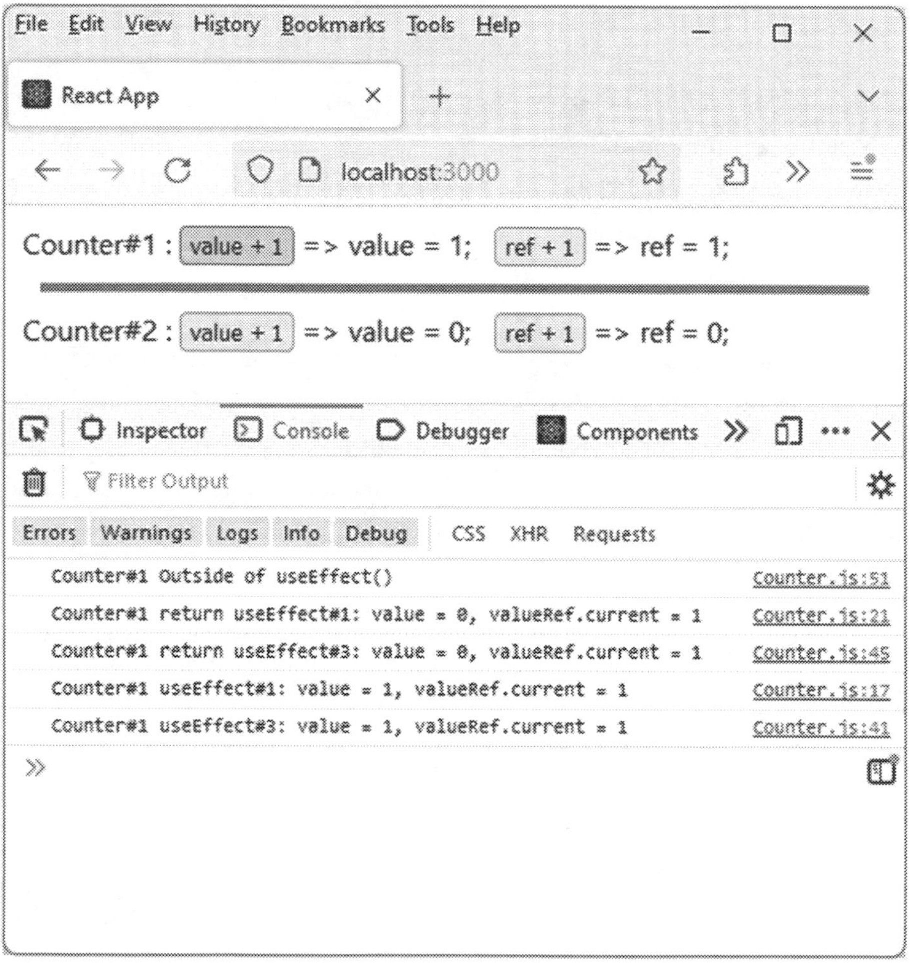

Figure 4-16. *Following the modification of a reactive variable "value"*

The executed effects are #1 and #3, which correspond to the effect executed in all cases (for effect #1, no expressed conditions) and the effect executed only if "valueRef.current" is modified (for effect #3, with conditions = [valueRef.current]). Indeed, we have modified the value of "valueRef.current" by clicking the "ref + 1" button previously.

Effect #2 is no longer executed, as it only concerns the initial display of the component (this is done using the parameter conditions = []).

We also observe that the functions indicated as the effect's return are executed before updating the component (value is 0 in the function and then becomes 1 afterward).

Let's clear the console messages once again, and then let's directly click the first "value + 1" button of the first counter. Thus, the value of "valueRef.current" is not modified here (Figure 4-17).

Figure 4-17. *Modifying "value" without modifying "valueRef. current"*

Here, we can observe that effect #3 is no longer executed, as the value of "valueRef.current" (which is part of the conditions for effect #3) is not modified. Only effect #1, executed in all cases, is executed here.

In summary, by adjusting the values in the conditions array of useEffect(), we control when effects are executed, taking into account the application's performance and specific needs:

- If no condition is specified: The effect runs after each display or update. This may result in reduced performance if the effect is not necessary with every component update.

- If an empty conditions array is provided: The effect runs only once after the initial render. This is useful for initializations but does not respond to updates.

- If a conditions array with values is provided: The effect runs on the initial display and when the values in the array change between updates. This optimizes the execution of effects by triggering them only when necessary, thus improving the application's performance.

Now that we have examined the useEffect() hook in detail, let's move on to using the useReducer() hook, which allows us to manage reactive variables in a different way than the previously used useState() hook.

Using the useReducer( ) Hook

The useReducer() hook is used to manage reactive variables in a component without using useState(). The useReducer() hook is employed when we can consider that the new value of one or more reactive variables depends on their previous value and an action to be performed.

For example, when incrementing a reactive variable "value" (as seen before), we can consider that the new value depends on the old value, upon which we perform the increment action. We could also provide a decrement action. Additionally, we could include in an additional parameter of the action the value by which the variable is incremented or decremented.

Let's use the Counter component, where we'll use the "value + 1" and "value - 1" buttons to increment or decrement the value of the reactive variable "value".

We will first use the useState() hook, followed by the useReducer() hook. This will allow us to observe the differences between the two approaches.

Step 1: Counter Component Using the useState( ) Hook

The following are the App and Counter components, using the useState() method to manage the reactive variable "value".

The App component is as follows:

App Component that displays the Counter components (file src/App.js)

```
import logo from './logo.svg';
import './App.css';
import Counter from "./Counter.js";

function App() {
  return (
    <>
      Counter#1 : <Counter />
      <hr style={{margin:'10px', height:'3px',
      backgroundColor:'gray'}}/>
      Counter#2 : <Counter />
    </>
  )
}

export default App;
```

The Counter component that uses the useState() method is as follows:

Counter component that displays buttons and the value of the reactive variable (file src/Counter.js)

```
import { useState } from "react";

function Counter() {
  const [value, setValue] = useState(0);

  function incrValue() {
    setValue(value+1);
  }

  function decrValue() {
    setValue(value-1);
  }

  return (
    <>
      <button onClick={incrValue}>value + 1</button>
        
      <button onClick={decrValue}>value - 1</button>
       
      =>
      value = {value};
    </>
  )
}

export default Counter;
```

We display the two buttons "value + 1" and "value - 1" that update the reactive variable "value". After clicking multiple times on the buttons of each component, we get the screen shown in Figure 4-18, demonstrating its proper functionality.

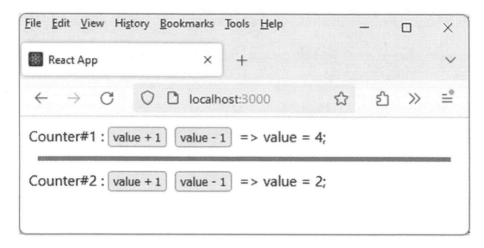

Figure 4-18. *Counters with increment and decrement buttons*

Now let's see how to achieve the same functionality using the useReducer() hook instead of useState().

Step 2: Counter Component Using the useReducer( ) Hook

The useReducer(reducer, initState) hook is used to manage the evolution of one or more reactive variables in the component that utilizes this hook. The reactive variables (one or more) managed by useReducer() are grouped into what is called the state, which corresponds to an object or a simple variable (as needed).

Let's explain the reducer and initState parameters of the useReducer(reducer, initState) method:

- The reducer parameter corresponds to a callback function in the form reducer(state, action). The reducer(state, action) function updates the state variable based on the action performed. The current state and the action to be performed are both passed as parameters to the callback function. The callback function returns the new state to be used once the action is performed.

- The initState parameter corresponds to the initial value of the state, which can be any value (numeric value, array, object, etc.).

When using the useReducer() hook, you first need to determine the variables that will be managed in the state and the actions that will cause them to progress. In our example, we can see that the state is represented by the single variable "value", while the actions that progress this variable are two actions named "INCR" (for incrementing the value) and "DECR" (for decrementing the value).

It is common to name actions as strings, but any other type of value would work as well, as we will see later.

Let's see how to use the useReducer() method in the Counter component. The App component remains the same as before.

Counter component using the useReducer() hook (file src/Counter.js)

```
import { useReducer } from "react";

function Counter() {
  const [value, dispatch] = useReducer(function(value,
  action) {
    if (action == "INCR") value += 1;
    if (action == "DECR") value -= 1;
    return value;
  }, 0);

  function incrValue() {
    dispatch("INCR");
  }
```

```
  function decrValue() {
    dispatch("DECR");
  }

  return (
    <>
      <button onClick={incrValue}>value + 1</button>
        
      <button onClick={decrValue}>value - 1</button>
       
      =>
      value = {value};
    </>
  )
}

export default Counter;
```

The useReducer() hook returns an array of two values:

- The first element of the array (at index 0) represents the new value of the state.

- The second element of the array (at index 1) represents a function (usually named dispatch) that allows you to update the state based on an action to be performed. The dispatch() function is used in the form dispatch(action).

In our example, we use the dispatch("INCR") method to increment the value and the dispatch("DECR") method to decrement the value. Calling these two methods triggers the execution of the reducer's callback function. The callback function uses the two parameters, value (the current value of the state) and action (the action to be executed to modify the state), to calculate and then return the new value of the state.

Let's verify that the functionality remains identical to the previous example that used useState() (see Figure 4-19).

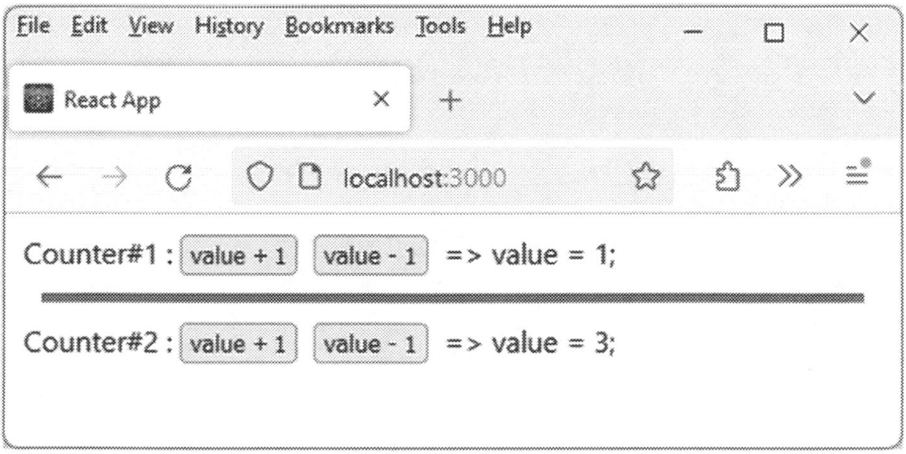

File Edit View History Bookmarks Tools Help   —   □   ×

React App   ×   +   ∨

← → C   ○ 🗋 localhost:3000   ☆ 🔖 » ≡

Counter#1 : [value + 1] [value - 1] => value = 1;
_____

Counter#2 : [value + 1] [value - 1] => value = 3;

Figure 4-19. *Counters using the useReducer() hook*

In this example, we used the useReducer() method instead of the useState() method. The useReducer() method offers more possibilities, particularly by allowing the use of a state that groups multiple values together, rather than just a single value as before.

Now, let's see how to manage state in the useReducer() hook when the state is represented as an object (which groups multiple properties) rather than a single value.

Step 3: Using the "state" Parameter as an Object

The "state" parameter used by the useReducer() method is often an object rather than a simple variable, as previously shown. This allows you to group multiple reactive variables within the same object, using object properties.

We can adapt the previous program to use a state object in the form { value1, value2, ... } instead of a simple variable "value".

Let's see how to proceed. The Counter component is modified:

Counter component using state as an object (file src/Counter.js)

```
import { useReducer } from "react";

function Counter() {
  const [state, dispatch] = useReducer(function(state,
  action) {
    if (action == "INCR") state.value += 1;
    if (action == "DECR") state.value -= 1;
    return { ...state };   // Definitely do not write return
    state; !!!
  }, {value : 0});

  function incrValue() {
    dispatch("INCR");
  }

  function decrValue() {
    dispatch("DECR");
  }

  return (
    <>
      <button onClick={incrValue}>value + 1</button>
        
      <button onClick={decrValue}>value - 1</button>
       
      =>
```

```
      value = {state.value};
    </>
  )
}

export default Counter;
```

The value of the reactive variable "value" is now stored in an object named "state" in the form { value }. The state contains only the "value" property since we are only managing this variable here, but it could contain other properties if needed.

Note that the state is initialized using this object as { value: 0 }, and access to the "value" property of the state is done everywhere using "state.value".

The interesting point to note is that the reducer returns the new value of the state, but it doesn't simply do "return state" as one might think. In fact, when you write "return state", you are returning a reference to the state object (i.e., its memory address), which is not modified in this case (it's the content of the memory address that is modified by "state.value += 1", not the address itself).

So, in order for React to realize that the state has changed (and refresh the displayed component), the memory address of the returned state object needs to be changed. This is achieved by using { ...state }, which creates a new memory object with the same content as the state object.

Step 4: Using the "action" Parameter as an Object

The "action" parameter is currently used as a string, such as "INCR" or "DECR". We can also use it as an object, which will allow us to provide additional parameters when using the dispatch() method.

For now, let's consider that the "action" parameter is an object. The name of the action to be performed corresponds, for example, to the "type" property of this object. It's a common practice to use the "type" attribute to contain the name of the action to be executed.

Let's modify the previous Counter component to use the "action" as an object { type }.

Counter component using the "action" as an object (file src/ Counter.js)

```
import { useReducer } from "react";

function Counter() {
  const [state, dispatch] = useReducer(function(state,
  action) {
    if (action.type == "INCR") state.value += 1;
    if (action.type == "DECR") state.value -= 1;
    return { ...state };    // Definitely do not write return
    state; !!!
  }, {value : 0});

  function incrValue() {
    dispatch({type : "INCR"});
  }

  function decrValue() {
    dispatch({type : "DECR"});
  }

  return (
    <>
      <button onClick={incrValue}>value + 1</button>
        
      <button onClick={decrValue}>value - 1</button>
       
      =>
```

```
    value = {state.value};
   </>
  )
}
```

```
export default Counter;
```

We verify that the Counter component works in the same way as before (see Figure 4-20).

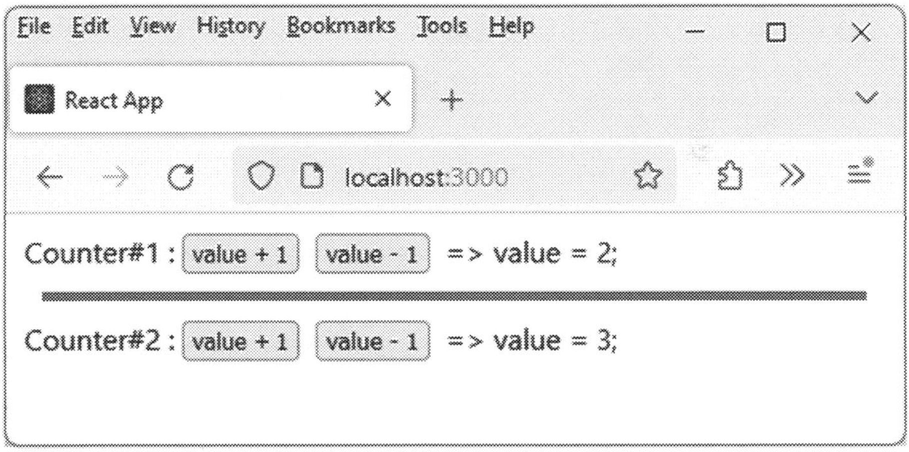

Figure 4-20. *The useReducer() hook uses action as an object*

The advantage of passing the action as an object is the ability to add other attributes to the action. For example, we can include the "value" attribute to indicate how much we want to increment or decrement the counter.

Thus, to increment the counter by 10 instead of 1, we would write dispatch({type: "INCR", value: 10}).

The Counter component is modified to use this new "value" attribute in the action:

Counter component using the "value" attribute in the dispatched action (file src/Counter.js)

```
import { useReducer } from "react";

function Counter() {
  const [state, dispatch] = useReducer(function(state,
  action) {
    if (action.type == "INCR") state.value += action.value;
    if (action.type == "DECR") state.value -= action.value;
    return { ...state };   // Definitely do not write return
    state; !!!
  }, {value : 0});

  function incrValue() {
    dispatch({type : "INCR", value : 10});
  }

  function decrValue() {
    dispatch({type : "DECR", value : 10});
  }

  return (
    <>
      <button onClick={incrValue}>value + 1</button>
        
      <button onClick={decrValue}>value - 1</button>
       
      =>
      value = {state.value};
    </>
  )
}

export default Counter;
```

And we get the screen shown in Figure 4-21.

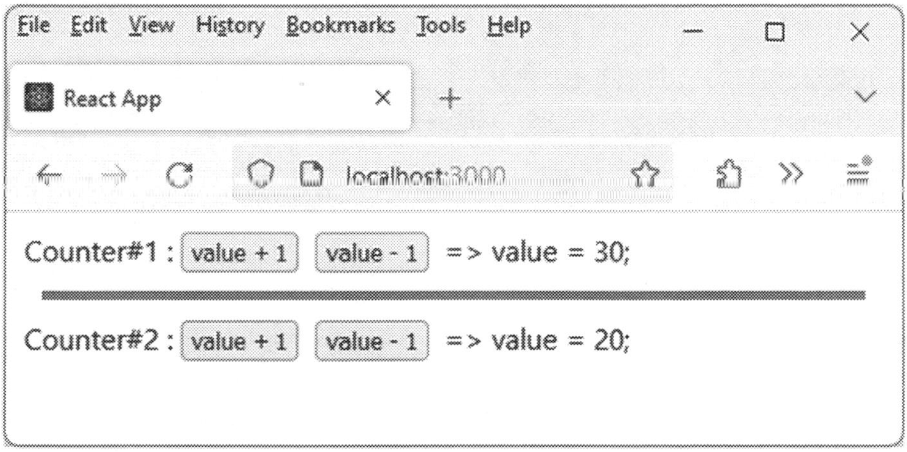

Figure 4-21. *The counter increments and decrements by 10*

Each click on one of the buttons results in an increment or decrement of 10. However, it would be better if the buttons displayed +10 instead of +1, and -10 instead of -1. Let's use the variables "valueIncr" and "valueDecr" to hold the increment and decrement steps.

Using the "valueIncr" and "valueDecr" variables to increment the state (file src/Counter.js)

```
import { useReducer } from "react";

function Counter() {
  const valueIncr = 10;  // +10 for each increment
  const valueDecr = 10;  // -10 for each decrement

  const [state, dispatch] = useReducer(function(state,
  action) {
    if (action.type == "INCR") state.value += action.value;
    if (action.type == "DECR") state.value -= action.value;
    return { ...state };   // Definitely do not write return
    state; !!!
```

```
}, {value : 0});

function incrValue() {
  dispatch({type : "INCR", value : valueIncr});
}

function decrValue() {
  dispatch({type : "DECR", value : valueDecr});
}

return (
  <>
    <button onClick={incrValue}>value + {valueIncr}</button>
      
    <button onClick={decrValue}>value - {valueDecr}</button>
     
    =>
    value = {state.value};
  </>
)
}

export default Counter;
```

The display is now as follows (Figure 4-22).

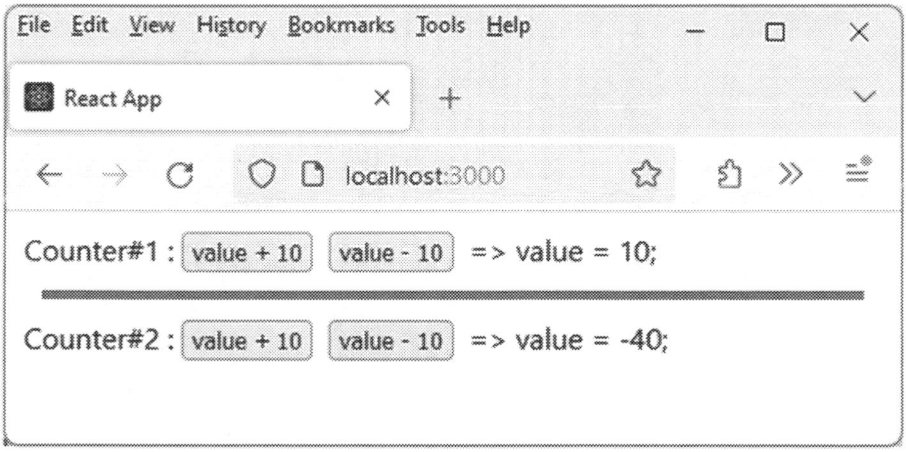

Figure 4-22. *Button texts are updated*

Other Hooks

We have seen the main hooks provided by React, namely, useState(), useEffect(), useRef(), useContext(), and useReducer().

React offers other hooks with specific functionalities. For example, useCallback() is used to optimize performance by avoiding the re-creation of functions on every component render, while useMemo() allows costly calculations to be memoized for improved performance.

Furthermore, for specific needs, it's possible to create your own custom hook, which we will explain now.

Creating Your Own Custom Hook

A hook is simply a function. It is recommended to prefix the function name with the word "use" to quickly distinguish the hooks used in our applications.

Since a hook is a function, it can accept 0 to n parameters and return the desired data. Often, a hook returns an array of data, such as with the useState() hook that returns the value of a reactive variable and the function to update it (written concisely as [count, setCount]).

A hook can also utilize other hooks (both those defined in React and those you've already created). Of course, the main rule of hooks (sequential usage) applies to our custom hooks as well.

The benefit of creating your own custom hook is to better structure the program that uses it and to be able to reuse it across multiple components.

Let's explore how to create and use our own custom hooks through a few examples.

Step 1: Creating a Hook to Limit Counter Value

We want to create a hook that limits the value of a counter.

The counters are similar to the ones displayed earlier, but now they have a maximum value which is passed in the "max" attribute of the Counter component.

When clicking the "value + 1" increment button, if the maximum value is reached, an error message appears and the increment becomes impossible. Clicking the "value - 1" decrement button removes the error message and decrements the counter value.

The functionality of the Counter component that uses this hook would be as follows. When the value of the first counter reaches 5 (the value of the "max" attribute), a message appears below it, and the counter is locked at that value (Figure 4-23).

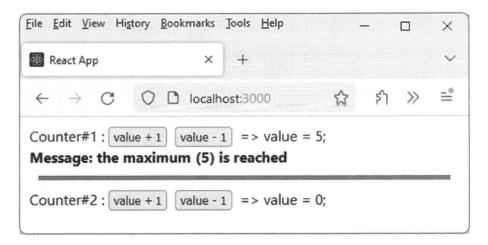

Figure 4-23. *The first counter displays a message and locks at value 5*

Both the App and Counter components are modified. The App component becomes the following, which includes the "max" attribute for each counter:

App component that displays the counters (file src/App.js)

```
import logo from './logo.svg';
import './App.css';
import Counter from "./Counter.js";

function App() {
  return (
    <>
      Counter#1 : <Counter max={5} />
      <hr style={{margin:'10px', height:'3px',
      backgroundColor:'gray'}}/>
      Counter#2 : <Counter max={10} />
    </>
  )
}

export default App;
```

The App component uses two counters. The first counter can increment up to a value of 5, while the second can increment up to a value of 10. This is indicated using the "max" attribute of the Counter component.

Now, we will create the useCounterMax(max) hook, where "max" represents the maximum value the counter should not exceed. We will write the hook in the useCounterMax.js file. This file will later be imported into components that want to use this hook.

To create this hook, we need to ask ourselves the following questions: What are its parameters, and what data or functionalities does it return? These are the questions you should always ask when creating your own hook.

Here are the answers to these two questions:

The parameter of the hook will be the maximum value to reach ("max" parameter).

The data returned by the hook could include

- The current value of the counter (stored in the "value" variable)

- An increment function for the "value" variable (named incr())

- A decrement function for the "value" variable (named decr())

- An optional error message, which will be displayed if the maximum counter value is reached (stored in the "error" variable)

These four pieces of data will be placed in an array that will be returned by the hook.

Here is the hook described in the useCounterMax.js file:

170

useCounterMax hook (file src/useCounterMax.js)

```
import { useState } from "react";

function useCounterMax(max) {
  const [value, setValue] = useState(0);
  function incr() {
    if (value < max) setValue(value+1);
  }
  function decr() {
    setValue(value-1);
  }
  var error = "";
  if (value >= max) error = `Message: the maximum (${max}) is
  reached`;
  return [value, incr, decr, error];
}

export default useCounterMax;
```

The hook creates a reactive variable "value" using the useState() hook. The functions incr() and decr() are created and modify the value of the "value" variable. The message associated with the "error" variable is set to an empty string ("") by default unless the counter value has reached the maximum. Finally, the array [value, incr, decr, error] is returned by the hook. This array can be used in the component that utilizes the hook.

Now, let's use the new hook in the Counter component:

Counter component that uses the useCounterMax() hook (file src/Counter.js)

```
import useCounterMax from "./useCounterMax";

function Counter({max}) {
  if (!max) max = 5;  // If max is not specified, it
  defaults to 5
```

```
  const [value, incr, decr, error] = useCounterMax(max);

  function incrValue() {
    incr();
  }

  function decrValue() {
    decr();
  }

  return (
    <>
      <button onClick={incrValue}>value + 1</button>
        
      <button onClick={decrValue}>value - 1</button>
       
      =>
      value = {value};<br/>
      <b>{error}</b>
    </>
  )
}

export default Counter;
```

The hook is imported into the component using the JavaScript import statement. The hook is used by calling it directly as useCounterMax(max). This call returns an array of four values in the order that the hook has positioned them in the returned array. These returned data can then be used in our Counter component.

Notice that the useState() hook is not used directly in the Counter component, but it is now used through the new useCounterMax() hook that we created.

Step 2: Creating a Hook to Force Component Update

We know that a component updates when one of its reactive variables is modified or when a parent component updates.

Sometimes it's useful to force a component update. For instance, when we previously used the useRef() hook, we noticed that updating the variable returned by useRef() didn't trigger a refresh of the containing component (see the section "Using the useRef() Hook"). In such cases, we could create a new hook that forces the component update.

Let's revisit the previously mentioned example that uses the following App and Counter components.

The original App component was as follows:

App component displaying two Counter components (file src/App.js)

```
import logo from './logo.svg';
import './App.css';
import Counter from "./Counter.js";

function App() {
  return (
    <>
      Counter#1 : <Counter />
      <hr style={{margin:'10px', height:'3px',
      backgroundColor:'gray'}}/>
      Counter#2 : <Counter />
    </>
  )
}

export default App;
```

The Counter component was as follows:

Updating variables defined by useState() and useRef() (file src/Counter.js)

```
import { useState, useRef } from "react";

function Counter() {
  const [value, setValue] = useState(0);
  const valueRef = useRef(0);

  function incrValue() {
    setValue(value+1);
  }

  function incrRef() {
    valueRef.current += 1;
  }

  return (
    <>
      <button onClick={incrValue}>value + 1</button>
       =>
      value = {value};
        

      <button onClick={incrRef}>ref + 1</button>
       =>
      ref = {valueRef.current};
        
    </>
  )
}

export default Counter;
```

When we run the application and click multiple times on the "ref + 1" button, the value of the "ref" reference doesn't update with each click. This is because you need to click the "value + 1" button, which updates the reactive variable "value" and triggers a refresh of the component (see Figure 4-24).

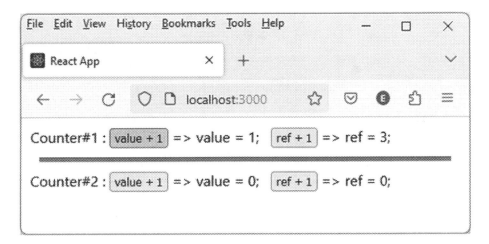

Figure 4-24. *The reference updates only if the "value" variable is updated*

We want to include a new "Refresh" button that updates the displayed "ref" references without modifying the reactive "value" variables.

For instance, you can click multiple times on the "ref + 1" buttons without clicking the "value + 1" buttons. Normally, the "ref" values are not modified with each click, but clicking the "Refresh" button automatically updates them (see Figure 4-25).

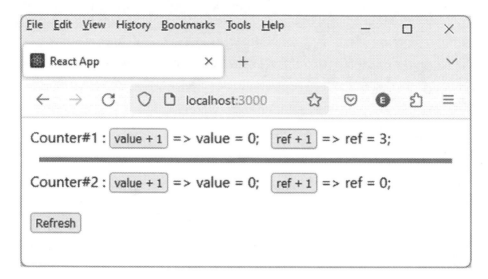

Figure 4-25. *Updating references by clicking the "Refresh" button*

To achieve this, we create a hook named, for example, useForceUpdate(). It returns the function forceUpdate(), which allows us to update the component in which it is called. If the component contains other components, they are also updated according to React's internal mechanisms.

Regarding the questions to consider when creating a new hook:

- What are its parameters for usage: No parameters are necessary here.

- What values does it return? It returns the forceUpdate() function, which allows for updating the component.

Now let's see how to write the content of the useForceUpdate() hook. The forceUpdate() function it returns should use a reactive variable that is modified with each call of the function. When a reactive variable is modified within a component, it triggers React to update the component (as well as any components included within it).

For this purpose, we use a simple boolean reactive variable that is inverted with each call: if it's true, we set it to false, and if it's false, we set it to true. Another approach could be using a counter that we increment with each call, achieving the same component refresh.

Description of the useForceUpdate() hook (file src/useForceUpdate.js)

```
import { useState, useEffect } from "react";

function useForceUpdate() {
  const [value, setBoolean] = useState(true);
  function forceUpdate() {
    setBoolean(!value);  // Invert the value of the reactive
    variable
  }
  return forceUpdate;
}

export default useForceUpdate;
```

The hook is now used in the App component, triggered by clicking the "Refresh" button.

Usage of the useForceUpdate() hook in the App component (file src/App.js)

```
import logo from './logo.svg';
import './App.css';
import Counter from "./Counter.js";
import useForceUpdate from "./useForceUpdate.js";

function App() {
  const forceUpdate = useForceUpdate();
  function refresh() {
    forceUpdate();
  }
```

```
  return (
    <>
      Counter#1 : <Counter />
      <hr style={{margin:'10px', height:'3px',
      backgroundColor:'gray'}}/>
      Counter#2 : <Counter />
      <br/><br/>
      <button onClick={refresh}>Refresh</button>
    </>
  )
}
```

```
export default App;
```

The Counter component remains unchanged.

Step 3: Creating a Hook to Retrieve the Previous Value of a Reactive Variable

The useState() hook allows us to know the current value of a reactive variable and set its next value. However, there are times when it's useful to know the previous value of this reactive variable.

For instance, let's use an input field in the Counter component. This field corresponds to a reactive variable that is modified with each character entered. The previous value of the reactive variable corresponds to the content of the field before the last character was introduced. For example, if we've entered the characters "abcde" in that order, the previous value of the field would be "abcd".

We display the previous content of the input field below the input field (Figure 4-26).

Figure 4-26. *Displaying the previous value of an input field*

For this purpose, we create the usePreviousState(state) hook, which returns the previous value of the reactive variable "state" associated with the content of the input field. The reactive variable "state" is modified each time a character is entered into the input field, using the onChange event.

Before describing the content of the usePreviousState() hook, let's first see how to use it in the Counter component.

Using the usePreviousState() hook to manage an input field (file src/ Counter.js)

```
import { useState, useRef } from "react";
import usePreviousState from "./usePreviousState";

function Counter() {
  const [value, setValue] = useState("");     // Current content
  of the input field
  const prevValue = usePreviousState(value); // Previous
  content of the input field

  function change(event) {
    var value = event.target.value;
```

```
    setValue(value);
  }

  return (
    <>
      Current Value : <input type="text" onChange={change} />
      <br />
      Previous value : {prevValue}
    </>
  )
}

export default Counter;
```

The App component that uses the Counter component is as follows:

App component that uses the Counter component (file src/App.js)

```
import logo from './logo.svg';
import './App.css';
import Counter from "./Counter.js";

function App() {
  return (
    <>
      <Counter />
    </>
  )
}

export default App;
```

Let's now write the content of the usePreviousState(state) hook.

To store the previous value of the "state" variable, we use a reference obtained through useRef(state) which will memorize it. Using a reference rather than a reactive variable to store it prevents an infinite loop: indeed, if we memorize a reactive variable by creating a new reactive variable, the creation of this reactive variable will trigger the creation of another one, and so on indefinitely, resulting in an infinite loop (this was explained in a previous section of this chapter).

Content of the usePreviousState(state) hook
(file src/usePreviousState.js)

```
import { useRef } from "react";

function usePreviousState(state) {
  var ref = useRef();
  var oldValue = ref.current;
  ref.current = state;
  return oldValue;
}

export default usePreviousState;
```

The variable "ref.current" holds the previous value of the reactive variable "state" passed as a parameter. This value is returned by the hook, and then the "state" variable is updated with the new value.

We verify that this works as indicated previously. However, a slight issue arises when attempting to clear the content of the field using, for example, the Backspace or Delete key. Indeed, by erasing all the content of the field, the last character is retained in the display of the previous value (Figure 4-27).

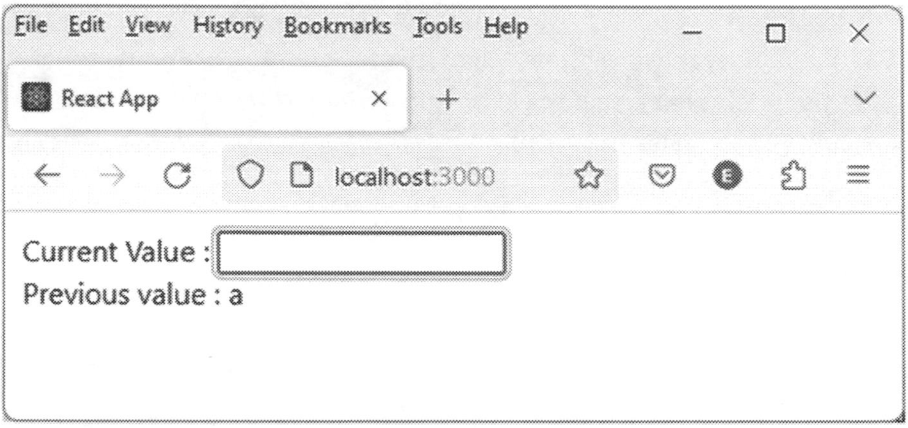

Figure 4-27. *The last character of the previous value doesn't get erased*

The issue stems from the fact that the Counter component doesn't update when we press Backspace or Delete for a second time when the input field is empty. Indeed, the reactive variable "value" associated with the field is no longer being modified since its value is already an empty string. However, it's only the modification of a reactive variable that triggers the component update.

To address this, let's use the previously mentioned "useForceUpdate()" hook. This hook enables component updates through its returned method, forceUpdate(). We should invoke this method when the Backspace or Delete key is pressed during input. For this purpose, we'll utilize the new onKeyDown event within the input field.

Using the useForceUpdate() hook during the onKeyDown event (file src/Counter.js)

```
import { useState, useRef } from "react";
import usePreviousState from "./usePreviousState";
import useForceUpdate from "./useForceUpdate";

function Counter() {
```

```
const [value, setValue] = useState("");    // Current content
of the input field
const prevValue = usePreviousState(value); // Previous
content of the input field
const forceUpdate = useForceUpdate();

function change(event) {
  var value = event.target.value;
  setValue(value);
}

function keydown(event) {
  if (event.key == "Backspace" || event.key == "Delete")
    forceUpdate();
}

return (
  <>
    Current Value : <input type="text" onChange={change}
    onKeyDown={keydown} /> <br />
    Previous value : {prevValue}
  </>
)
}

export default Counter;
```

We verify that the previous value is reset to "" (empty) upon the second press of the Backspace key when the input field is empty (Figure 4-28).

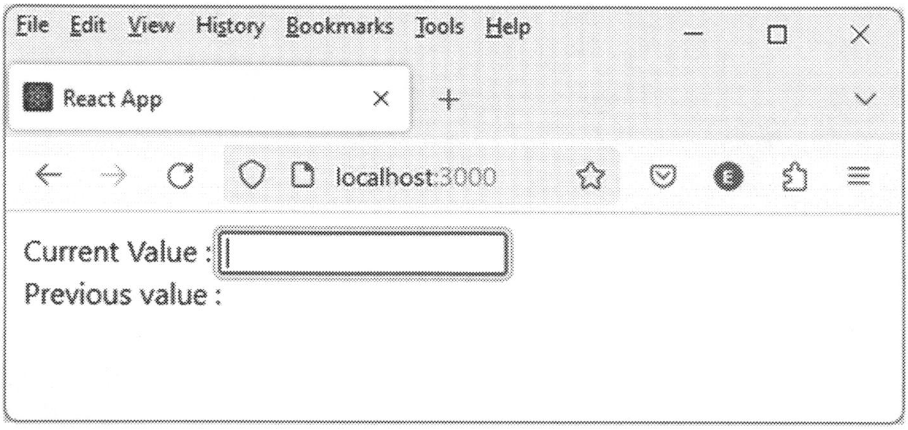

Figure 4-28. *The previous value is now erased if the input field is empty*

Step 4: Creating a Hook to Fetch Data from a Server

Here's a highly useful hook that enables communication with any server. We will make use of the fetch(url) method in JavaScript, which allows us to retrieve data from a server based on the provided URL parameter. The purpose of this hook, named useFetch(url) in this context, will be to fetch data from a server and provide it to requesting components. As an example, we'll utilize the service provided by the server `https://restcountries.com`. The URL `https://restcountries.com/v3.1/all` allows us to retrieve JSON-formatted details about different countries worldwide.

In Figure 4-29, we display this URL, which lets us visualize the characteristics of the first country returned by the service—Barbados, in this case. It's possible that Barbados might not be the first country displayed when you use this URL, as the server's display order of countries could have changed since then.

To display the result in the format shown in Figure 4-29, in Firefox, click the Raw Data tab and then the Pretty Print button.

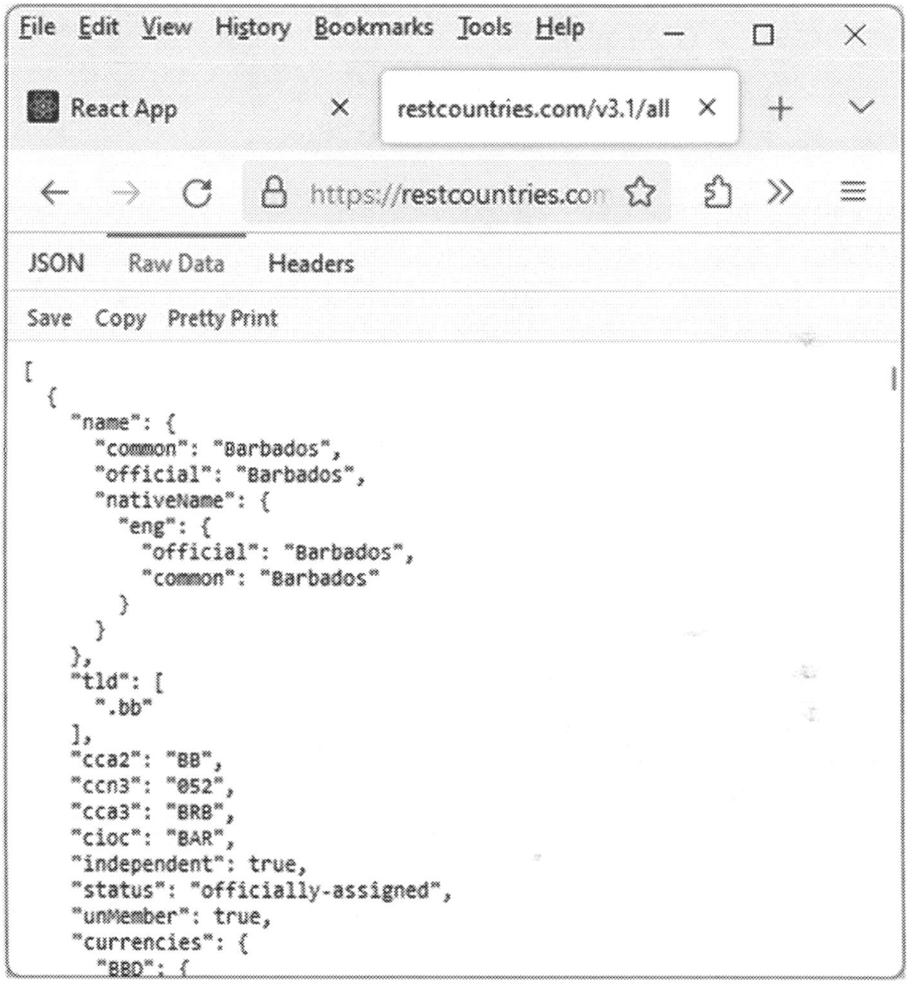

Figure 4-29. *Using the* `https://restcountries.com/v3.1/all` *service*

To employ the useFetch() hook within our React programs, we will do so using the Countries component, which we will develop gradually according to our needs.

The Countries component is utilized within the App component (in place of the previous Counter component):

App component utilizing the Countries component (file src/App.js)

```
import logo from './logo.svg';
import './App.css';
import Countries from "./Countries.js";

function App() {
  return (
    <>
      <Countries />
    </>
  )
}
```

```
export default App;
```

Now, let's describe the useFetch(url) hook, which allows us to retrieve the data provided by the specified URL and return either that data or an error. The return value of this hook is a tuple [data, error] containing the data (data) or the error (error). Each of these two elements is set to null if it doesn't exist.

The useFetch.js file outlines the useFetch() hook:

useFetch() hook (file src/useFetch.js)

```
import { useState, useEffect } from "react";

const useFetch = function(url) {
  const [data, setData] = useState("");
  const [error, setError] = useState("");

  useEffect(function() {
    fetch(url)
      .then((res) => res.text())
```

```
      .then((data) => setData(data.toString()))
      .catch((err) => setError(err.toString()))
    ;
  }, [url]);

  return [data, error];
};

export default useFetch;
```

First, let's explain the fetch(url) method. It returns a Promise object, allowing the invocation of the first then() method. The res.text() method also returns a Promise object, enabling the invocation of the second then() method. The catch() method specified at the end is used to handle errors.

Next, let's explain the two reactive variables, data and error, used here. Why use reactive variables in this case?

Suppose we don't use reactive variables. The fetch() method makes a server call that returns data or an error, with a certain latency. If the variables returned by the useFetch() method are not reactive, the returned values will be the initial values, not the ones obtained in response from the server (as the latter arrive after the useFetch() function returns these values). While the server data will eventually arrive, the component using them won't see their modification because the associated variables are not reactive.

If the returned variables are reactive, their subsequent modification will be considered in the component using them, resulting in an update of the server-obtained data in the component.

Finally, let's explain why we use the useEffect() hook. It allows us to condition the execution of the fetch(url) function on the modification of the url parameter. If the component using useFetch(url) is refreshed, the fetch() method will not be used again because the url parameter remains unchanged.

Now, let's write the Countries component that uses the useFetch() hook.

Countries component using the useFetch() hook (file src/Countries.js)

```
import useFetch from "./useFetch";

function Countries() {
  const [data, error] = useFetch("https://restcountries.com/
  v3.1/all");

  return (
    <>
      { (!error && !data) ? <>Waiting</> :
        (error ? <>{error}</> : <>{data}</>)
      }
    </>
  )
}
```

```
export default Countries;
```

If the variables data and error are empty, we display the message "Waiting". Otherwise, we display the error message returned by error, or the data returned by data.

As explained earlier, the fact that the data and error variables are reactive in the useFetch() hook allows the Countries component, which uses this hook, to benefit from their reactivity and display their value changes if they occur.

Upon launching the program, the screen in Figure 4-30 is displayed.

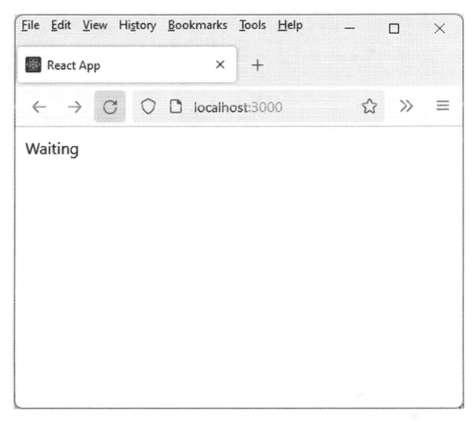

Figure 4-30. *The program is awaiting data from the server*

When the data is received from the server, it is displayed instead of the waiting message (Figure 4-31).

Figure 4-31. *The data has been received from the server*

We have seen how to obtain information from the server. Let's now see how to format it on the displayed page.

Step 5: Creating a Hook for Data Formatting

The information returned by the server was previously displayed directly on the HTML page (in the form of JSON strings) without any formatting. Now, we want to display only the name of each country, in alphabetical order of names.

To achieve this, we create a new hook named useCountries(). This new hook will use the previous useFetch() hook. It will be directly used within the Countries component, replacing useFetch().

useCountries() hook (file src/useCountries.js)

```
import useFetch from "./useFetch";

const useCountries = function() {
  const [data, error] = useFetch("https://restcountries.com/
  v3.1/all");
  var countries;
  if (data) {
    countries = JSON.parse(data).map(function(elem) {
      return elem.name.common;
    });
    countries = countries.sort((n1, n2) => (n1 > n2));
  }
  return countries;
};

export default useCountries;
```

The JavaScript-defined method JSON.parse() allows us to transform a string of characters into a JSON-format object, in this case, an array of elements. The map() method enables us to iterate through the elements of this array and return the name of each country, recorded in the name. common property of each element. The resulting array of returned names is then sorted in alphabetical order using the sort() method. Subsequently, the array is returned by the hook to be used within the Countries component.

The Countries component, which utilizes the new hook, becomes as follows:

Countries component using the useCountries() hook (file src/Countries.js)

```
import useCountries from "./useCountries";
import { Fragment } from "react";

function Countries() {
  const countries = useCountries();

  return (
    <>
      { (!countries) ? <>Waiting</> :
        (
          <>{
            countries.map(function(name, index) {
              return <Fragment key={index}>{name}<br/>
              </Fragment>
            })
          }</>
        )
      }
    </>
  )
}
export default Countries;
```

Once the countries have been passed to the browser, they are displayed on the HTML page in alphabetical order (Figure 4-32).

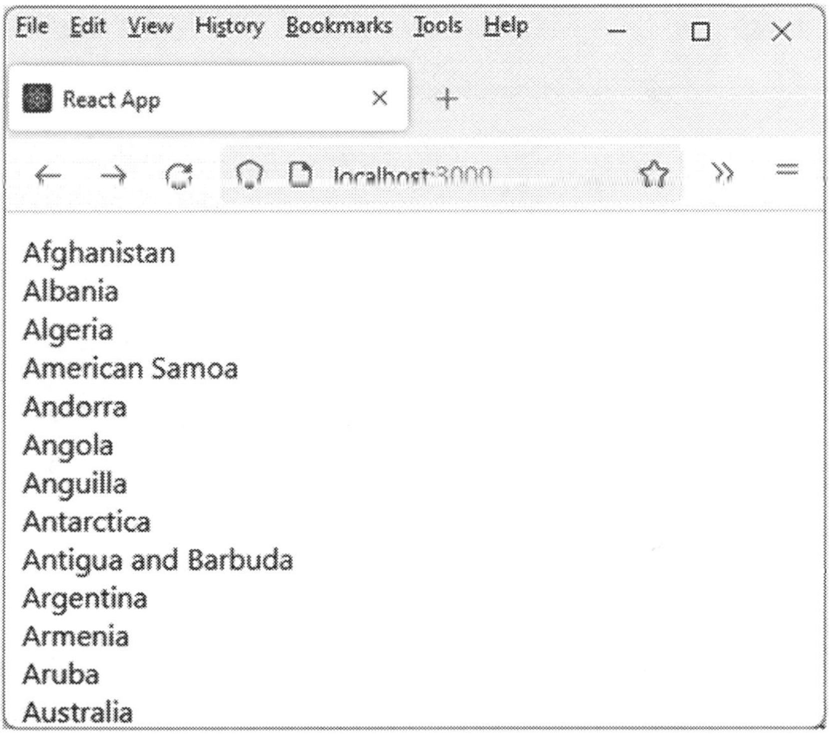

Figure 4-32. *List of countries displayed in alphabetical order*

Now let's see how to further enhance the Countries component by allowing the filtering of countries based on their names.

Step 6: Creating a Hook That Filters the Displayed Data

We aim to improve the useCountries() hook by passing a string of characters that should be contained in the names of the countries to be displayed. For this purpose, we use an input field displayed above the list of countries. As we type in the input field, the list of countries is updated to display only those whose names contain the entered string (see Figure 4-33).

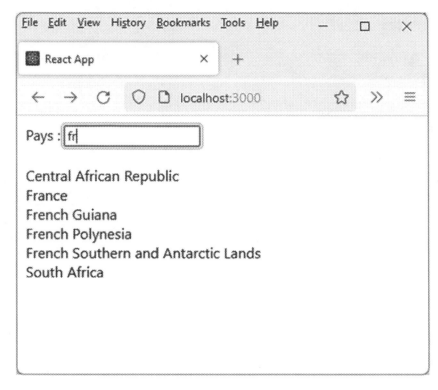

Figure 4-33. *List of countries containing the string "fr"*

The useCountries() hook is modified to use the parameter "name, which will be used to filter the country names containing the string specified by the "name" parameter.

useCountries(name) hook (file src/useCountries.js)

```
import useFetch from "./useFetch";

const useCountries = function(name) {
  const [data, error] = useFetch("https://restcountries.com/
  v3.1/all");
  var countries;
  if (data) {
```

```
  countries = JSON.parse(data).map(function(elem) {
    return elem.name.common;
  });
  countries = countries.sort((n1, n2) => (n1 > n2));
  if (name) countries = countries.filter((n) =>
  n.toUpperCase().includes(name.toUpperCase()));
  }
  return countries;
};

export default useCountries;
```

The filter() method defined on the JavaScript Array class allows us to retain only the country names in the "countries" array that contain the specified "name" string. To avoid issues with capitalization, the names are compared after converting them to uppercase.

The Countries component uses the "name" parameter provided by the hook. This "name" parameter is specified in the attributes of the Countries component. The "name" parameter will be passed to the Countries component through the App component, which displays the Countries component.

Countries component using the name attribute (file src/Countries.js)

```
import useCountries from "./useCountries";
import { Fragment } from "react";

function Countries({name}) {
  const countries = useCountries(name);

  return (
    <>
      { (!countries) ? <>Waiting</> :
        (
          <>{
```

```
        countries.map(function(name, index) {
          return <Fragment key={index}>{name}<br/>
          </Fragment>
        })
      }</>
    )
  }
  </>
 )
}
```

```
export default Countries;
```

Now, we need to modify the App component to enable the entry of letters from the country names to be displayed. We insert an <input> element into the JSX code of the App component.

App component enabling country name filtering (file src/App.js)

```
import logo from './logo.svg';
import './App.css';
import Countries from "./Countries.js";
import { useState } from "react";

function App() {
  const [name, setName] = useState("");
  function change(event) {
    var value = event.target.value;
    setName(value);
  }

  return (
    </>
      Country: <input type="text" onChange={change}/>
      <br/><br/>
```

```
      <Countries name={name} />
    </>
  )
}
```

```
export default App;
```

We create the new reactive variable "name" within the App
component. It is passed in the attributes of the Countries component.
As the variable is reactive, the Countries component will be updated
whenever the value of the variable changes, since this reactive variable is
passed to it in the attributes.

Conclusion

The fourth day of our React learning journey was dedicated to the
use of hooks. We learned how hooks can be used to manage state and
component life cycle more efficiently.

Hooks are a powerful tool for managing state and component life cycle
in React. We are now equipped to use hooks to make our code cleaner,
more efficient, and more easily maintainable. We are ready to continue our
React learning journey and explore further the possibilities offered by this
exciting JavaScript library, using all the accumulated knowledge to create a
task list management application with React.

CHAPTER 5

Day 5: Practical Application— Managing a Task List with React

In this chapter, we will put into practice all the knowledge gained in the previous days by creating an application that manages a task list.

We will use components, events, and hooks to create a dynamic and interactive user interface that allows users to add, edit, and delete tasks in a list. We will also see how to manage data in a React application using state and form handling.

By creating this application, you will not only practice the concepts learned in the previous chapters, but you will also discover how to put all these elements together to create a complete React application, step by step.

Ready to put your React skills into practice? Let's get started!

Application Screens

Let's start by displaying the screens of our application to explain its functionality. We will write the React code in the remainder of this chapter.

Initially, the task list is empty. The "Add Item" button in Figure 5-1 allows you to insert a new item into the list with each click.

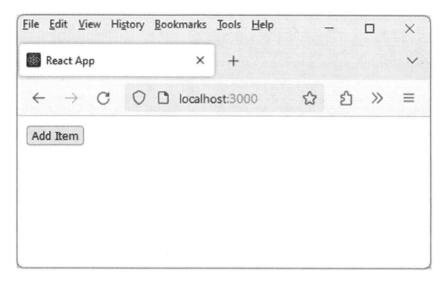

Figure 5-1. *Application launch screen*

Let's click the "Add Item" button multiple times (three times here, see Figure 5-2).

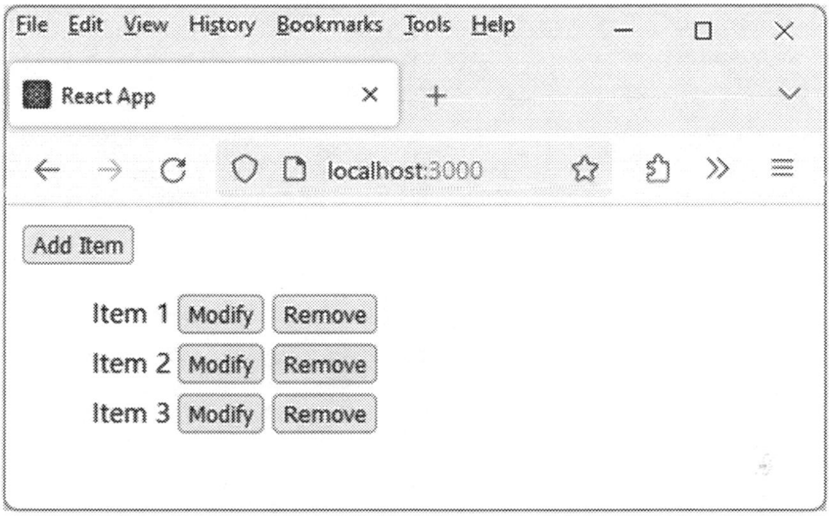

Figure 5-2. *After three clicks on the "Add Item" button*

Each inserted item is assigned an index (starting from 1) in the list (Item 1, Item 2, etc.). A "Remove" button and a "Modify" button are added next to each item in the list.

Let's click the "Modify" button on the second row (Item 2). The text of the item is replaced by an input field, where the cursor blinks to allow editing (see Figure 5-3).

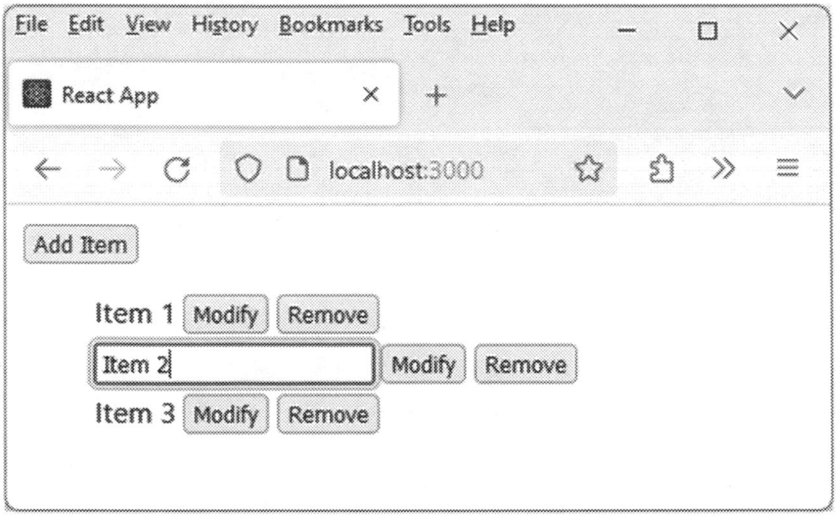

Figure 5-3. *The second item in the list can be modified*

Let's edit the text in the input field by typing "Modified Item 2" (Figure 5-4).

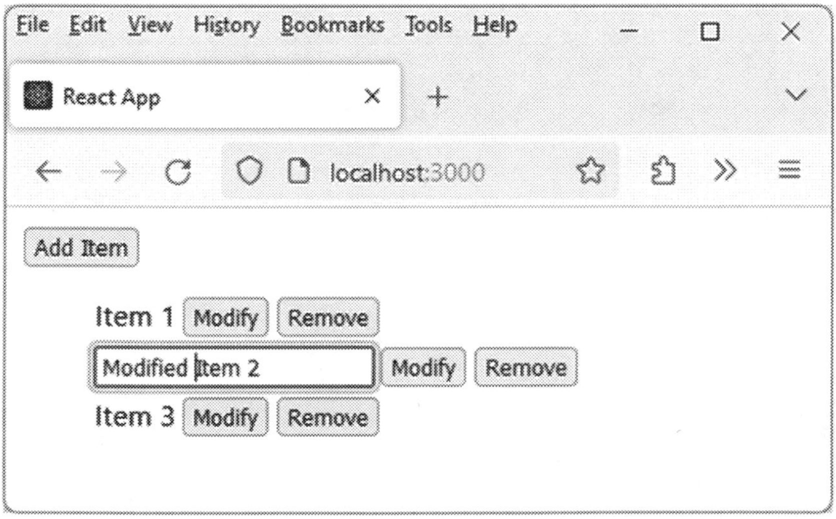

Figure 5-4. *Editing a list item*

To apply the modification of the item, you need to exit the input field by clicking elsewhere on the page (Figure 5-5).

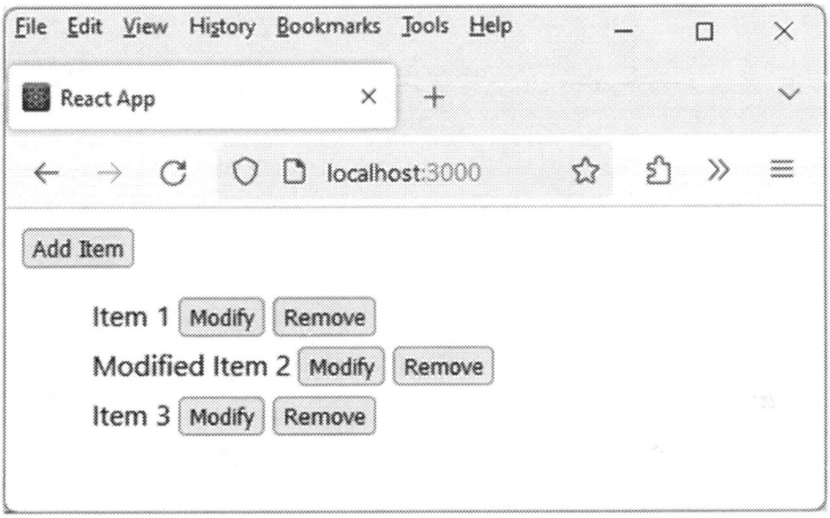

Figure 5-5. *Modification of the item is applied*

Finally, let's click the "Remove" button on the first and third rows (Figure 5-6).

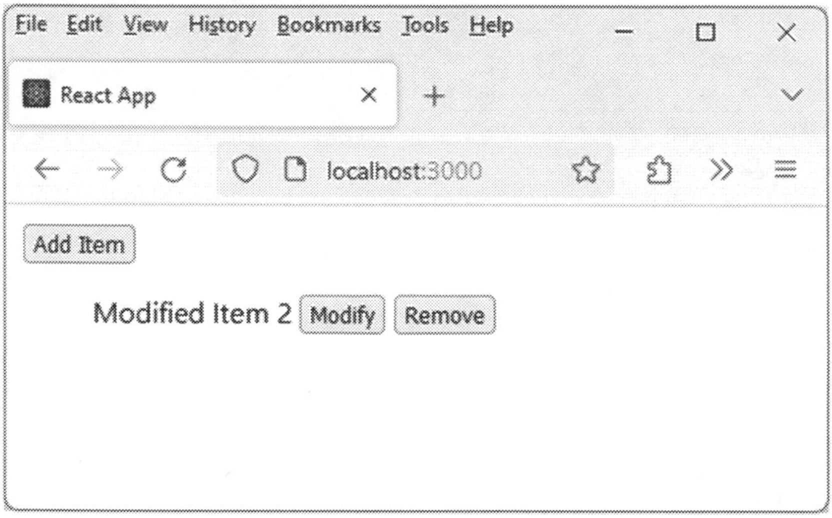

Figure 5-6. *After removing the first and last items*

Now let's see how to create this application using React.

Creating the Application with create-react-app

We create the "list" application by entering the command "create-react-app list" in a command prompt. We will use the directory structure created by this command, especially by using or creating new files in the "src" directory of the created application.

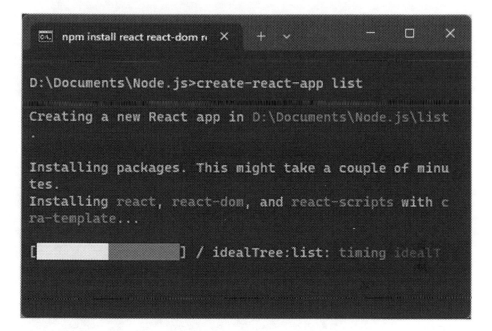

Figure 5-7. *Creation of the "list" application*

Once the application is finished being created, the commands to start the server are displayed at the end of the application creation process (Figure 5-8).

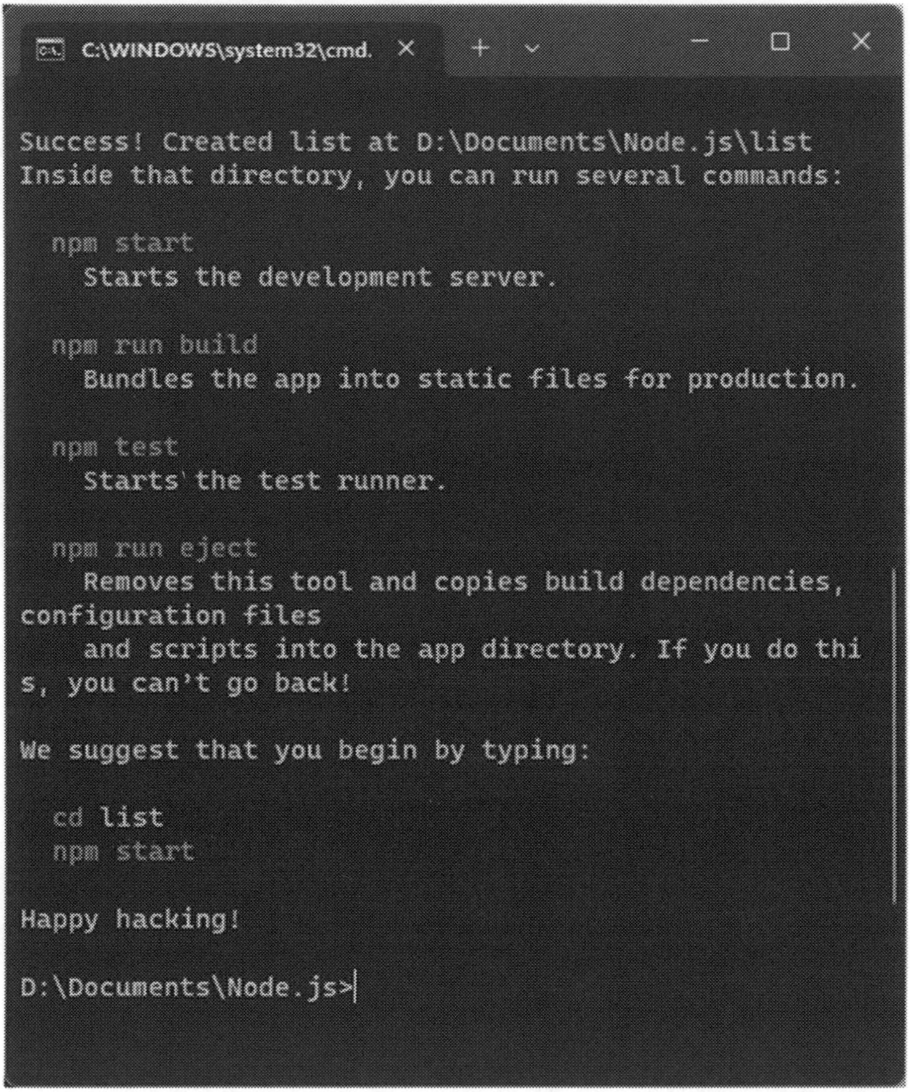

```
C:\WINDOWS\system32\cmd.    ×    +  ∨              —   ☐    ✕

Success! Created list at D:\Documents\Node.js\list
Inside that directory, you can run several commands:

  npm start
    Starts the development server.

  npm run build
    Bundles the app into static files for production.

  npm test
    Starts the test runner.

  npm run eject
    Removes this tool and copies build dependencies,
configuration files
    and scripts into the app directory. If you do thi
s, you can't go back!

We suggest that you begin by typing:

  cd list
  npm start

Happy hacking!

D:\Documents\Node.js>|
```

Figure 5-8. *End of application creation*

To start the application located at the URL http://localhost:3000, simply enter the commands "cd list" and then "npm start".

Breaking Down the Application into Components

With the previously listed application screens, we can already identify the main components of our application:

- The App component is the primary application component that contains the other components.

- The Items component corresponds to the list of items.

- The Item component corresponds to an individual item in the list.

Therefore, the App component will encompass the "Add Item" button and the Items component.

To manage the list of items, we will use a reactive variable "items", which will be an array containing the name of each item in the list.

This reactive variable "items" will be updated whenever an item is inserted, removed, or modified. Since it needs to be accessible when clicking the "Add Item" button located in the App component, we will integrate this reactive variable into the App component.

Now, let's explore how to execute the various list manipulations, specifically

- Adding an item to the list

- Removing an item from the list

- Modifying an item in the list

Let's start by studying how to add an item to the list.

Adding an Item to the List

We will implement the App, Items, and Item components as described earlier. These components will be adjusted as we incorporate additional functionalities. At this point, our focus will be on handling the click event of the "Add Item" button.

These files are situated in the "src" directory of the "list" application. We will modify the App.js file of the App component and generate the necessary files for the Items and Item components.

The App component is outlined as follows:

App component (file src/App.js)

```
import logo from './logo.svg';
import './App.css';
import { useState } from "react";
import Items from "./Items";

function App() {
  const [items, setItems] = useState([]);

  function add() {
    var item = "Item " + (items.length + 1);
    items.push(item);
    setItems([...items]);
  }

  return (
    <>
      <button onClick={add}>Add Item</button>
      <Items items={items} />
    </>
  );
}

export default App;
```

Explanation:

- We use the useState() hook to define the reactive variable "items", initialized to an empty array [ ]. This variable will hold strings associated with the items in the list, constructed in the format "Item" + (items. length + 1). The list is initially empty, hence the initialization to [ ].

- To modify the content of this reactive variable, we use the setItems() method returned by useState(). When modifying the list using setItems(), we pass a new array as a parameter, as updating the reference of the array triggers the variable update, not modifying its content. Hence, we use [...items] to create a new array (with a different memory reference) containing the same content.

- The JSX code returned by the App component includes the "Add Item" button, which has an onClick event to handle button clicks, and also includes the list of items to display, associated with the Items component. We pass the list of items contained in the reactive variable "items" to this component. The Items component will use this "items" parameter to display the list of items it contains.

Note that the returned JSX code must always have a root element that encompasses all other elements. Since the <button> and <Items> elements don't have a common root element, we add a fictitious one using <> and </>.

We also modify the App.css file that contains the application styles. We simply want to add a margin of 10 pixels between the displayed elements and the window edges.

Application styles (file src/App.css)

```
body {
  margin : 10px;
}
```

Let's move on to describing the other components of the application. Let's start with the Items component, which is used to display the list as a whole.

The Items component is as follows:

Items component (file src/Items.js)

```
import Item from "./Item";

function Items({ items }) {
  return (
    <ul style={{ listStyleType: "none" }}>
      {items.map(function (item, index) {
        return <Item key={index} name={item} />;
      })}
    </ul>
  );
}

export default Items;
```

In the parameter of the Items component, we specify the name of the items attribute that is passed to it, in the form of {items}. This items parameter is then used through the map() method to return the JSX code to be displayed for each item in the list.

For each item in the list, we return a new component, named Item here, to which we pass the text of the item to display (in the item attribute) and the index of the item in the list (in the key attribute), as we know that React requires each element in a displayed list to have a key attribute with a unique value in the list.

Now let's see the description of the Item component, which is the final component of our application. This Item component displays an item from the list using the "name" attribute (containing the text of the item to display) that is passed to it.

The Item component is as follows:

Item component (file src/Item.js)

```
function Item({ name }) {
  return (
    <li style={{ marginTop: "5px" }}>
      <span>{name}</span>
       
      <button>Modify</button>
       
      <button>Remove</button>
    </li>
  );
}

export default Item;
```

The Item component displays the text of the list item (contained in the "item" attribute) and the two Modify and Remove buttons, which are currently inactive.

Let's verify that we can add items to the list by clicking the Add Item button (Figure 5-9).

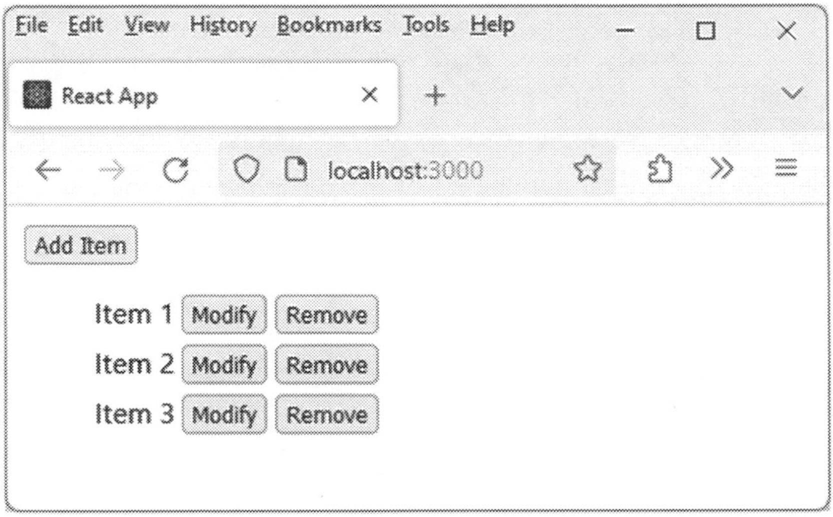

Figure 5-9. *Insertion of three items into the list*

Insertion into the list works. Now, let's see how to remove an item from the list.

Removing an Item from the List

Removing an item from the list is done by clicking the Remove button within the Item component. We will create a method named remove() in the Item component that will be responsible for removing the item from the list.

When removing an item from the list, the reactive variable "items" within the App component needs to be updated. This update can only be achieved by using the setItems() function returned by useState() in the App component.

Therefore, the Item component needs to be able to access and update this reactive variable "items", which is located in a parent component (the App component). To achieve this, we will pass the setItems() method as an attribute. We will introduce a new attribute named, for example, setItems, with a value of {setItems}. This attribute will be passed from the App component to the Items component, and then to the Item component. This will allow the Item component to update the reactive variable "items" located within the App component.

It's worth noting that we could also use the useContext() hook, which enables data sharing between a component and its children, whether direct or nested. This would eliminate the need to pass the setItems() update function to the other components.

Furthermore, we need to transmit the index of the item to be deleted from the list. To achieve this, we use the "index" attribute within the Item component. This "index" attribute is set within the Items component when creating each Item component.

Please observe that the item's index is also used with the "key" attribute, but this attribute is internal to React and cannot be directly used within our components.

The App component is modified to incorporate the setItems attribute when creating the Items component within the App component.

The App component now becomes as follows:

App component (src/App.js file)

```
import logo from './logo.svg';
import './App.css';
import { useState } from "react";
import Items from "./Items";

function App() {
  const [items, setItems] = useState();

  function add() {
    var item = "Item " + (items.length + 1);
    items.push(item);
```

```
    setItems([...items]);
  }

  return (
    <>
      <button onClick={add}>Add Item</button>
      <Items items={items} setItems={setItems} />
    </>
  );
}

export default App;
```

The Items component is modified to take into account the setItems attribute that is passed to it, and to add the index attribute when creating each Item component.

The Items component now becomes as follows:

Items component (src/Items.js file)

```
import Item from "./Item";

function Items({ items, setItems }) {
  return (
    <ul style={{ listStyleType: "none" }}>
      {items.map(function (item, index) {
        return <Item key={index} name={item} index={index}
        setItems={setItems} />;
      })}
    </ul>
  );
}

export default Items;
```

Finally, the Item component is modified to accommodate the handling of the Remove button using the added remove() method within the Item component. The index and setItems attributes are passed to this component.

The Item component now becomes as follows:

Item component (src/Item.js file)

```
function Item({name, index, setItems}) {
  function remove() {
    setItems(function(items) {
      items = items.filter(function(item, i) {
        if (index == i) return false;
        else return true;
      });
      return [...items];
    });
  }
  return (
    <li style={{marginTop:"5px"}}>
      <span>{name}</span>
       
      <button>Modify</button>
       
      <button onClick={remove}>Remove</button>
    </li>
  );
}
export default Item;
```

The function setItems(), passed through the component's attributes, becomes accessible within the Item component. The reactive variable "items" is also accessible here by using the callback function within setItems(callback).

To remove an item from the list, it's sufficient to update the reactive variable "items" using the setItems() function. The filter() method of the Array class allows us to return a new array, where we return true for the elements we want to keep and false for the elements we want to remove. In this case, we are keeping all elements except the one with the specified index attribute.

Furthermore, to trigger an update of the reactive variable, we need to return a new reference of it, hence the creation of a new array using [... items]. This creates a new array with a new memory address, containing the same elements as before.

Note   The filter() method in JavaScript returns a new array with a new memory reference. Therefore, it's not necessary here to use array destructuring with return [...items], and we can simply use the instruction return items.

Let's verify that this works. We create four items in the list; then we remove the second and third items. Only the first and fourth items remain (see Figure 5-10).

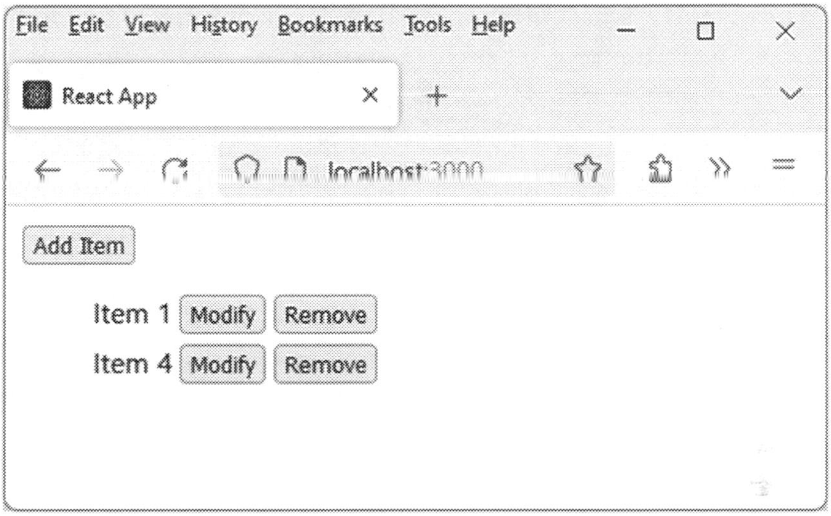

Figure 5-10. *Removing items from the list*

We have seen how to add and remove items from the list. Now let's see how to modify them.

Modifying an Item in the List

Modifying an item in the list is a bit more complex to implement. Let's proceed through different steps to understand the requirements.

First, we need to transform the text of the list item into an input field that initially contains the text of the list item. The changes to the program will take place within the Item component.

Step 1: Modifying the Item

To display either an input field or plain text (depending on whether the Modify button has been clicked or not), we use a new reactive variable named "modifyOn", which is a boolean variable set to true if the input field is displayed (Modify button clicked) or false if only the plain text is displayed (Modify button not clicked). This reactive variable "modifyOn" is initialized to false and becomes true when the Modify button is clicked.

Using a reactive variable allows us to dynamically change the display when the variable is modified, which is the role of a reactive variable.

Therefore, the Item component becomes as follows. It will be further modified in the following pages to progressively reach the final goal for better understanding.

Item component (src/Item.js file)

```
import { useState } from "react";

function Item({name, index, setItems}) {
  const [modifyOn, setModifyOn] = useState(false);

  function remove() {
    setItems(function(items) {
      items = items.filter(function(item, i) {
        if (index == i) return false;
        else return true;
      });
      return [...items];
    });
  }

  function modify() {
    setModifyOn(!modifyOn);
  }

  return (
    <li style={{marginTop:"5px"}}>
      { modifyOn ?
          <input type="text" value={name} /> :
```

```
        <span>{name}</span>
    }
     
    <button onClick={modify}>Modify</button>
     
    <button onClick={remove}>Remove</button>
  </li>
 );
}
```

```
export default Item;
```

As explained earlier, we use the reactive variable "modifyOn" initialized to false. This variable is modified when clicking the Modify button, within the modify() function triggered by the Modify button click.

The JSX code of the component utilizes the value of the reactive variable "modifyOn" to display either the input field or the text element. In both cases, we display the value of the item {name} within the input field or the text element.

Let's execute this program while also displaying the console using F12, which contains any potential error messages. We insert an item and then click the Modify button (Figure 5-11).

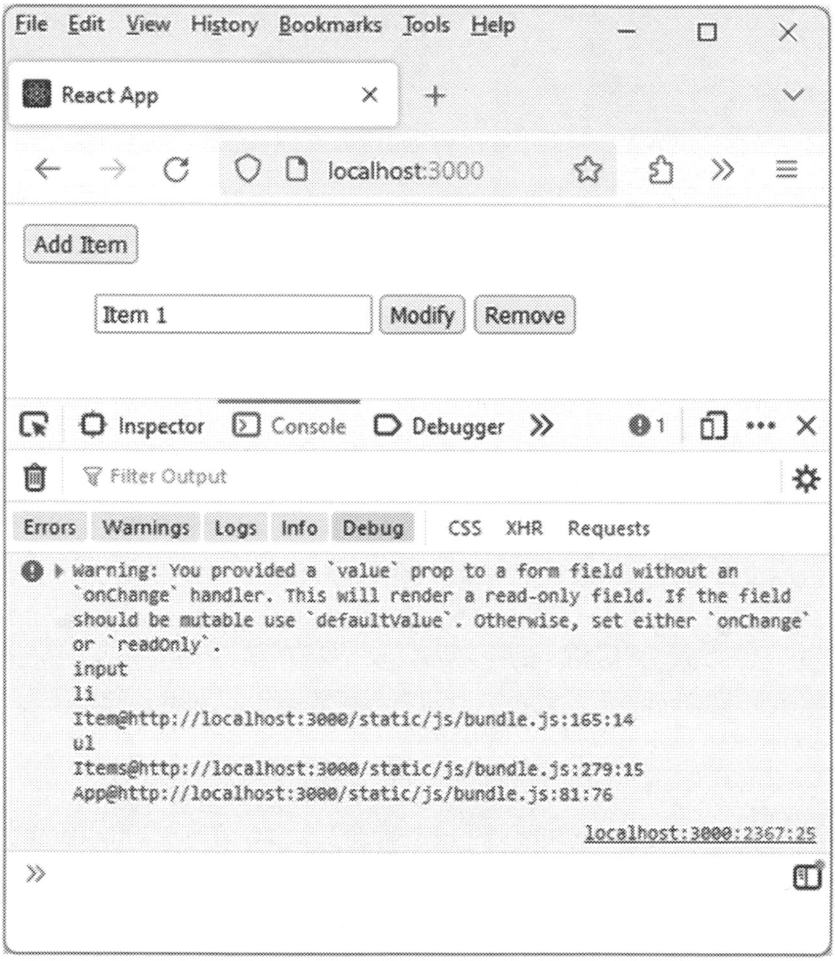

Figure 5-11. *Clicking the Modify button*

We observe that clicking the Modify button toggles the display between the input field and the element as text. Indeed, modifying a reactive variable (here, modifyOn) within the component triggers the component's update and therefore its re-rendering. The message in the console (in this case, a warning) informs us that we need to implement the onChange event in the input field. Since we initialized the "value" property of this field, we also need to handle its potential changes.

Let's implement the handling of the onChange event in the input field. For now, we are displaying its content in the console (i.e., the value of event.target.value).

Handling the onChange event in the input field (src/Item.js file)

```
import { useState } from "react";

function Item({name, index, setItems}) {
  const [modifyOn, setModifyOn] = useState(false);

  function remove() {
    setItems(function(items) {
      items = items.filter(function(item, i) {
        if (index == i) return false;
        else return true;
      });
      return [...items];
    });
  }

  function modify() {
    setModifyOn(!modifyOn);
  }

  function change(event) {
    console.log(event.target.value);
  }
```

```
  return (
    <li style={{marginTop:"5px"}}>
      { modifyOn ?
          <input type="text" value={name}
          onChange={change} /> :
          <span>{name}</span>
      }
       
      <button onClick={modify}>Modify</button>
       
      <button onClick={remove}>Remove</button>
    </li>
  );
}

export default Item;
```

Let's type characters into the input field, for example, "a", then "b", then "c", then "d", and finally "e" (see Figure 5-12).

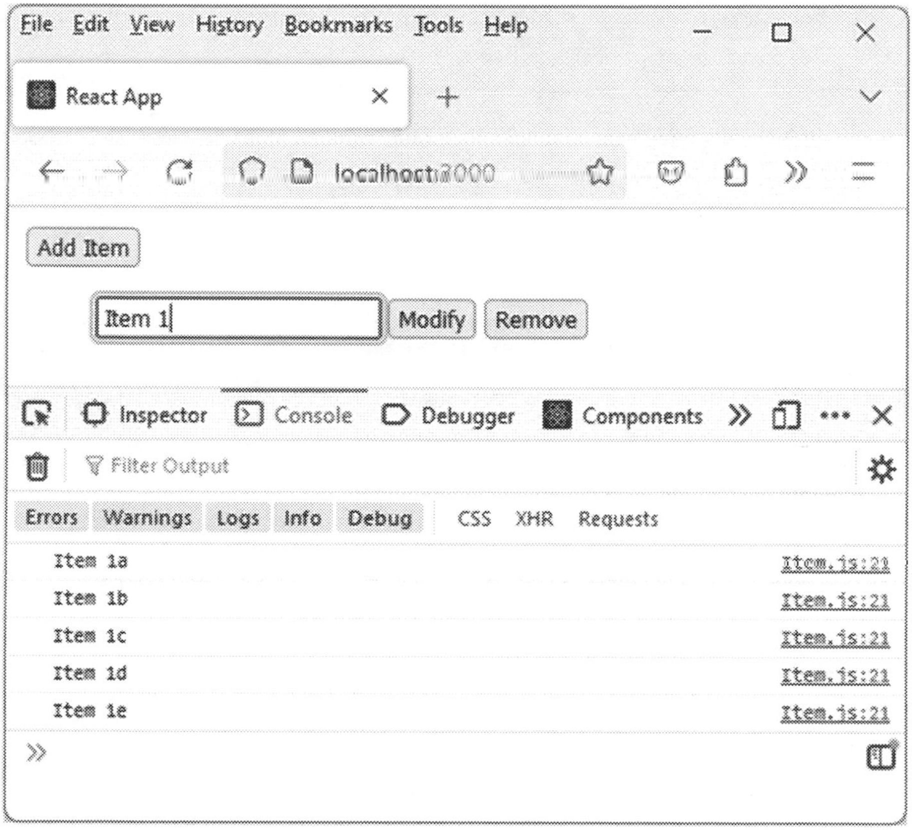

Figure 5-12. *Modifying the input field: it isn't updated*

We can see that the characters are captured correctly by the onChange event but are not visible in the input field, which remains unchanged. Indeed, to modify the input field, we need to update the component's display, as the input field's "value" property is initially set to the initial value, which is the text of the item, that is, {name}. The "value" property of the input field needs to reflect the current value in the input field for each typed character.

To achieve this, we use a new reactive variable, here named "text", which will be used to store and display the value in the input field.

Let's use the reactive variable "text" within the Item component to handle the modification of the input field:

Modifying the input field (src/Item.js file)

```
import { useState } from "react";

function Item({name, index, setItems}) {
  const [modifyOn, setModifyOn] = useState(false);
  const [text, setText] = useState(name);

  function remove() {
    setItems(function(items) {
      items = items.filter(function(item, i) {
        if (index == i) return false;
        else return true;
      });
      return [...items];
    });
  }

  function modify() {
    setModifyOn(!modifyOn);
  }

  function change(event) {
    console.log(event.target.value);
    setText(event.target.value);
  }
```

```
return (
  <li style={{marginTop:"5px"}}>
    { modifyOn ?
        <input type="text" value={text}
        onChange={change} /> :
        <span>{text}</span>
    }
     
    <button onClick={modify}>Modify</button>
     
    <button onClick={remove}>Remove</button>
  </li>
);
}

export default Item;
```

The "text" variable is updated as characters are typed, triggered by the onChange event. This "text" variable is reactive and is the one displayed in the JSX code instead of the "name" variable, which is not reactive. This enables the updating of the text displayed in the input field for each typed character.

Let's display the input field and enter characters as before. We can see that the typed characters are correctly displayed in both the console and the input field (Figure 5-13).

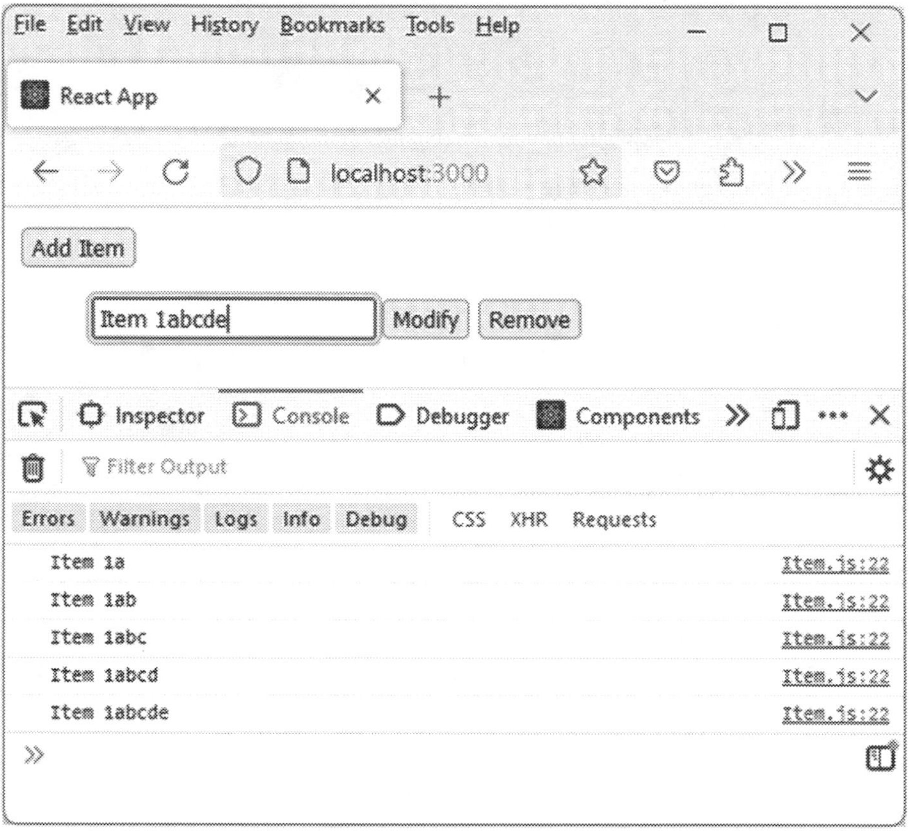

Figure 5-13. *Modifying the input field: it's finally updated*

Next, let's proceed to the next step, which involves considering the modification of the input field.

Step 2: Validation of the Modification

The input field has become editable. Now we need to handle leaving the input field (onBlur event) by redisplaying the text element (in place of the input field) and updating this element in the list of items (in the reactive "items" variable):

- To restore the text element in place of the input field,
  simply set the reactive variable "modifyOn" to false.

- To modify the value of the element in the reactive
  "items" variable, update the element in the "items"
  array and then return a new array using return
  [...items].

Let's modify the Item component to incorporate these changes.

Item component (src/Item.js file)

```
import { useState } from "react";

function Item({name, index, setItems}) {
  const [modifyOn, setModifyOn] = useState(false);
  const [text, setText] = useState(name);

  function remove() {
    setItems(function(items) {
      items = items.filter(function(item, i) {
        if (index == i) return false;
        else return true;
      });
      console.log(items);
      return [...items];
    });
  }

  function modify() {
    setModifyOn(!modifyOn);
  }
```

```
  function change(event) {
    // console.log(event.target.value);
    setText(event.target.value);
  }

  function blur(event) {
    // Remove the input field
    setModifyOn(false);
    // Modify the item in items variable
    setItems(function(items) {
      items[index] = event.target.value;
      return [...items];
    });
  }

  return (
    <li style={{marginTop:"5px"}}>
      { modifyOn ?
          <input type="text" value={text} onChange={change}
          onBlur={blur} /> :
          <span>{text}</span>
      }
       
      <button onClick={modify}>Modify</button>
       
      <button onClick={remove}>Remove</button>
    </li>
  );
}

export default Item;
```

We have also added a console log displaying the reactive variable "items" after each removal of an item from the list. This helps verify if the removal is still functioning correctly.

Let's insert three items into the list and then remove the first item from the list. Observe the value of the reactive variable "items" displayed in the console and compare it with the list displayed on the page (see Figure 5-14).

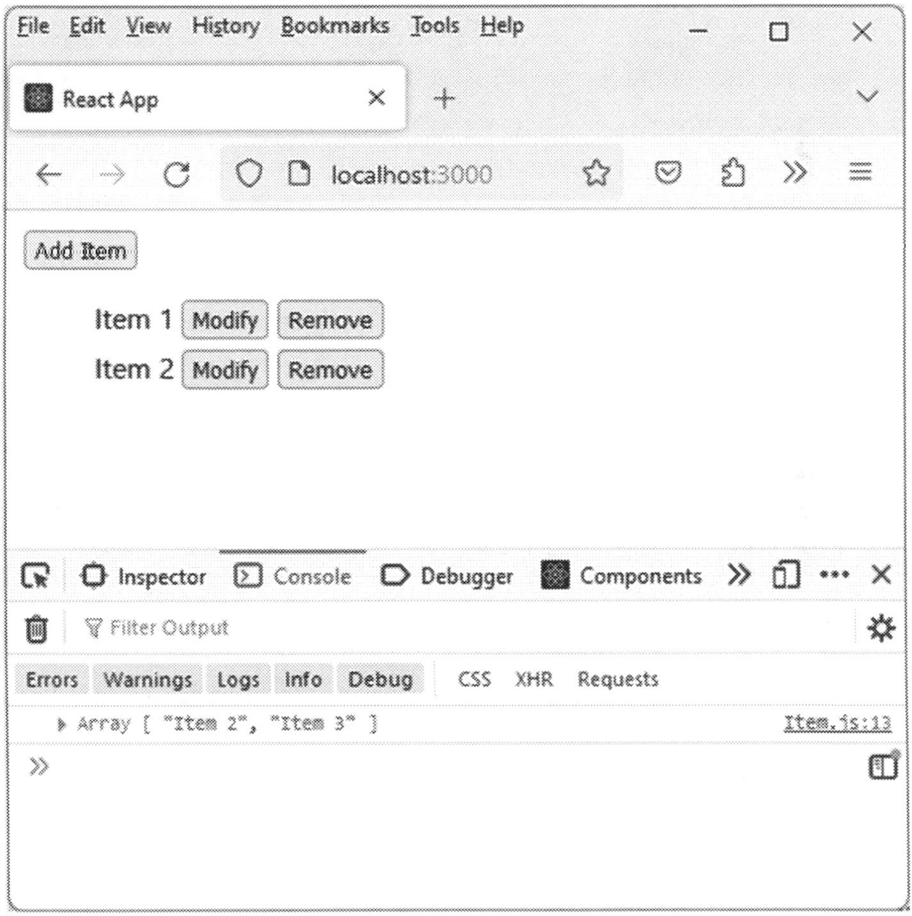

Figure 5-14. *List after removing the first item*

We observe that the "items" variable in the console matches the expected outcome, but the display is not updated! It still includes the first list item even though it should have been removed.

What could be the reason for this inconsistency?

In React, the "key" attribute is used to help React identify each item in a list. When React updates the contents of a list, it compares the new list to the old one based on the keys ("key" attributes) of the list items. This enables React to determine which item was added, removed, or modified. It's important for each list item to have a unique key, as this allows React to distinguish each item and update them correctly in case of changes. If two items have the same key, React won't know which one to update, potentially leading to unexpected behavior.

Furthermore, each list item should always maintain the same key it was previously assigned. This ensures that React doesn't create new items every time a list is updated, which could lead to performance issues.

In summary, the use of unique and consistent keys in lists is crucial to ensure React functions properly when updating list content.

Therefore, the program needs to be modified so that each list item is associated with a unique key, which cannot be the index of the item in the list. Using the index as the key would not be unique in cases where the list is modified due to item removal.

Step 3: Assigning a Unique Value for the "key" Attribute

To assign a unique value for the "key" attribute of each list item, we use a reactive variable named "key", which will be updated using the setKey(value) method returned by useState().

An item placed in the "items" array will now be an object { name, key }, allowing us to know the unique "key" associated with each list item.

The App component is thus modified:

App component (src/App.js file)

```
import logo from './logo.svg';
import './App.css';
import { useState } from "react";
import Items from "./Items";

function App() {
  const [items, setItems] = useState();
  const [key, setKey] = useState(1);

  function add() {
    var name = "Item " + key;  // Item 1, Item 2, ...
    setKey(key+1);  // Obtaining the next key associated with
    the list item
    items.push({name, key});
    setItems([...items]);
    console.log(items);
  }

  return (
    <>
      <button onClick={add}>Add Item</button>
      <Items items={items} setItems={setItems} />
    </>
  );
}

export default App;
```

The Items component needs to be modified to accommodate the new structure of the "items" array.

Items component (src/Items.js file)

```
import Item from "./Item";

function Items({ items, setItems }) {
  return (
    <ul style={{ listStyleType: "none" }}>
      {items.map(function (item) {
        var {name, key} = item;
        return <Item key={key} name={name} index={key}
        setItems={setItems} />;
      })}
    </ul>
  );
}

export default Items;
```

The "key" attribute, now used in the Item component, is unique for each list item. The "index" attribute is also set to the value of the "key" key.

The Item component is also modified so that modifications or removals of an item are performed based on the value of the "key" key associated with the item (set in the "index" attribute).

Why use two attributes ("key" and "index") to refer to the same value?

React requires, for its internal functioning, the use of the "key" attribute, which must have a unique value for each item in the list. However, this "key" attribute cannot be used directly in our programs, hence the use of another attribute named "index" here, which holds the same value. It is this "index" attribute that we can manipulate in our programs to perform the operations.

Item component (src/Item.js file)

```
import { useState } from "react";

function Item({name, index, setItems}) {
  const [modifyOn, setModifyOn] = useState(false);
  const [text, setText] = useState(name);

  function remove() {
    setItems(function(items) {
      items = items.filter(function(item) {
        // Removal of the item where index = item.key
        if (index == item.key) return false;  // Remove
        else return true;  // Keep
      });
      console.log(items);
      return [...items];
    });
  }

  function modify() {
    setModifyOn(!modifyOn);
  }

  function change(event) {
    // console.log(event.target.value);
    setText(event.target.value);
  }

  function blur(event) {
    // Remove the input field
    setModifyOn(false);
    // Modify the item in items variable
    setItems(function(items) {
```

```
      items = items.map(function(item) {
        // Modification of the item where index = item.key
        if (index == item.key) item.name = event.target.value;
        return item;
      });
      return [...items];
    });
  }

  return (
    <li style={{marginTop:"5px"}}>
      { modifyOn ?
          <input type="text" value={text} onChange={change}
          onBlur={blur} /> :
          <span>{text}</span>
      }
       
      <button onClick={modify}>Modify</button>
       
      <button onClick={remove}>Remove</button>
    </li>
  );
}

export default Item;
```

Let's verify that these modifications produce the expected changes. We create three list items and then remove the first one. The previous bug has now been resolved (see Figure 5-15).

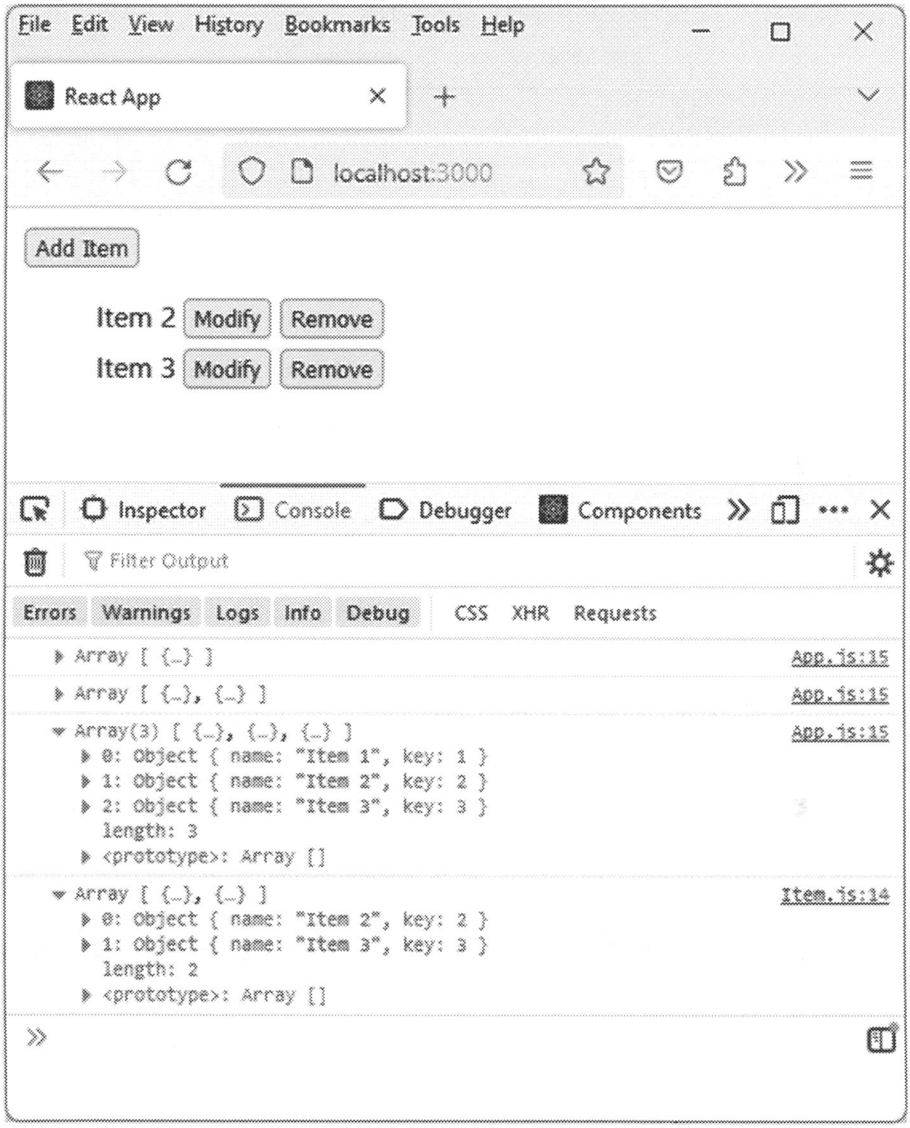

Figure 5-15. *Correct display after modification and removal of an item*

In this example, we have demonstrated the importance of assigning a unique value to the "key" attribute in list items within React. This value must be unique regardless of the existing or future items in the list.

Step 4: Obtaining Focus Directly on the Input Field

Finally, we need to ensure that the input field receives focus directly when clicking the Modify button, rather than having to click inside the field to give it focus.

To achieve this, we will use the useRef() hook, which we explained in the previous chapter. We will set the "ref" attribute in the <input> element of the JSX code in the Item component. The "ref" attribute should have the value obtained from calling the useRef() hook earlier in the component's code.

For example, if we define const refInput = useRef(), we will use ref={refInput} in the JSX code of the <input> element. The focus() method can then be called using the statement refInput.current.focus().

When to use this instruction?

This instruction should be used when the input field appears in the Item component, that is, after clicking the Modify button. React allows performing actions after each component's rendering or update using the useEffect() hook, which is called at that moment. Indeed, transforming a text field into an input field in a component corresponds to updating the component.

However, it's necessary to ensure that the component's update involves displaying the input field (the Item component can be displayed or updated without the input field being present). To achieve this, simply test within the useEffect() hook whether the value of refInput.current exists. If it exists, it means the input field is present during rendering, and we can use the focus() method on this variable. Otherwise, an error occurs when rendering the items because the input field does not exist.

Let's use the useRef() and useEffect() hooks to give focus to the input field when it is created.

Item component (src/Item.js file)

```
import { useState, useEffect, useRef } from "react";

function Item({name, index, setItems}) {
  const [modifyOn, setModifyOn] = useState(false);
  const [text, setText] = useState(name);
  const refInput = useRef();

  useEffect(function() {
    // If the input field exists, give it focus
    if (refInput.current) refInput.current.focus();
  });

  function remove() {
    setItems(function(items) {
      items = items.filter(function(item) {
        // Removal of the item where index = item.key
        if (index == item.key) return false;  // Remove
        else return true;  // Keep
      });
      console.log(items);
      return [...items];
    });
  }
```

```
function modify() {
  setModifyOn(!modifyOn);
}

function change(event) {
  // console.log(event.target.value);
  setText(event.target.value);
}

function blur(event) {
  // Remove the input field
  setModifyOn(false);
  // Modify the item in items variable
  setItems(function(items) {
    items = items.map(function(item) {
      // Modification of the item where index = item.key
      if (index == item.key) item.name = event.target.value;
      return item;
    });
    return [...items];
  });
}

return (
  <li style={{marginTop:"5px"}}>
    { modifyOn ?
        <input type="text" value={text} onChange={change}
        onBlur={blur} ref={refInput} /> :
        <span>{text}</span>
    }
     
    <button onClick={modify}>Modify</button>
     
```

```
      <button onClick={remove}>Remove</button>
    </li>
  );
}
export default Item;
```

Let's click the Modify button of the first item in the list, and the focus is directly given to the input field (Figure 5-16).

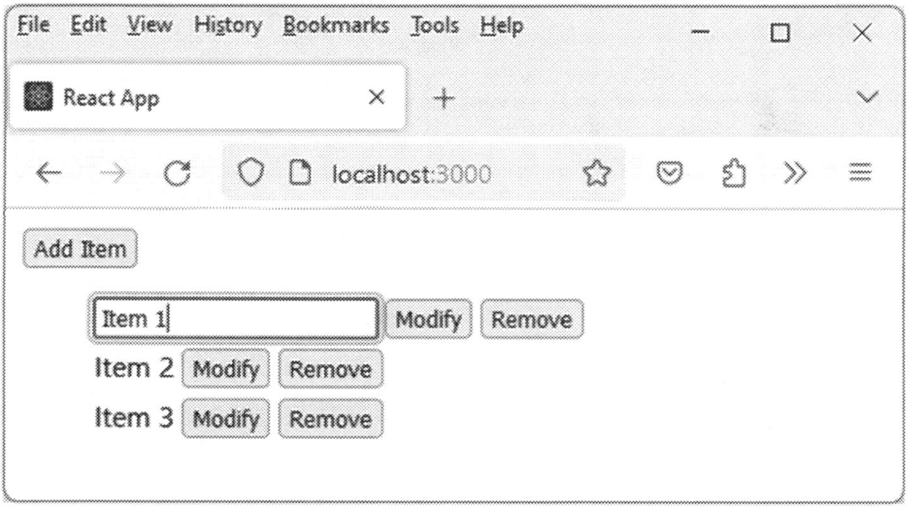

Figure 5-16. *The input field receives focus directly*

Conclusion

This chapter has been an exploration of creating and managing lists with React. We learned how to handle list items with unique keys and how to dynamically update a list in response to user events.

The skills acquired in this chapter are highly useful for creating various types of web applications, including enterprise dashboards, to-do list apps, or ecommerce applications. By utilizing these skills, you're capable of creating dynamic and interactive lists, thereby enabling users to efficiently manipulate and visualize data.

We have now completed our study of React in just 5 days! You have the essential elements in this book to effectively use React, having understood its internal functioning. If this book has satisfied you, I kindly ask you to post a comment on the social media platforms you use. In addition to purchasing this book, that would be my best reward!

In the next chapter, we provide you with a summary of the JavaScript features we've used previously.

CHAPTER 6

JavaScript Reminders

Here's the final chapter, "JavaScript Reminders," of our book *Master React in 5 Days*. Before diving into the world of React, it's important to recall the basics of JavaScript. This chapter aims to help you remember and brush up on the key concepts of JavaScript that are used throughout the book.

We will cover key concepts such as variables, arrays, objects, arrow functions, and modules. We will also explore more advanced concepts like asynchronous functions.

- If you're already familiar with JavaScript, this chapter will help you recall and ensure you have the necessary foundation to understand the code examples in React.

- If you're new to the world of JavaScript, this chapter will provide you with a solid groundwork to grasp the concepts we'll be using throughout the book.

Ready to strengthen your JavaScript knowledge? Let's get started!

Using the "let" and "var" Keywords in JavaScript

In JavaScript, "let" and "var" are two keywords used for declaring variables. The main difference between the two lies in the variable's scope.

© Eric Sarrion 2023
E. Sarrion, *Master React in 5 Days*, https://doi.org/10.1007/978-1-4842-9855-8_6

The "var" keyword has function scope, meaning the variable is accessible inside the function in which it is declared, as well as everywhere inside that function.

For example:

Using "var" to define a variable

```
function example() {
  var x = 10;
  if (true) {
    var x = 20; // The variable x is accessible inside the
    function example()
  }
  console.log(x); // Displays 20
}
```

In this example, the variable x is declared inside the function example(), but it is also accessible within the "if" block, because "var" has function scope. Therefore, writing "var x = 20;" does not create a new variable, as the variable x was declared earlier and is directly accessible within the "if" block. By writing "var x = 20;", we are only modifying the value of the previously created variable.

On the other hand, the "let" keyword has block scope, which means the variable is accessible only within the block in which it is declared and in all nested blocks inside that block.

For example:

Using "let" to define a variable

```
function example() {
  let x = 10;
  if (true) {
```

```
    let x = 20; // The variable x is accessible only within the
    "if" block
  }
  console.log(x); // Displays 10
}
```

In this example, the variable "x" is declared inside the function example(). However, the second declaration of x inside the "if" block creates a new variable "x", which is accessible only within that block. The variable x outside the "if" block retains its initial value of 10.

In summary, the main difference between "let" and "var" is the variable's scope: "var" has function scope, and "let" has block scope. It is generally recommended to use "let" rather than "var" in JavaScript code, as it provides better control over variable scope and helps avoid accidental variable reuse across different blocks.

Using the "const" Keyword in JavaScript

In JavaScript, the "const" keyword is used to declare a variable that cannot be reassigned after its initial value has been assigned. It creates a variable with a constant, unchangeable reference to a value. This means that once a value is assigned to a "const" variable, you cannot reassign it to a different value later in the code.

Here's an explanation of how the "const" keyword works and its key characteristics:

When declaring a variable using "const", you must immediately assign a value to it. Unlike the "var" or "let" keywords, you cannot declare a "const" variable without initializing it.

Declaration and initialization

```
const pi = 3.14159;
```

Once a value is assigned to a "const" variable, its value cannot be changed. Attempting to reassign a "const" variable will result in an error.

Value immutability

```
const pi = 3.14159;
pi = 3.14; // This will result in an error
```

Like variables declared with "let", "const" variables are block-scoped. They are only accessible within the block (enclosed by curly braces) where they are defined.

Block scope

```
if (true) {
  const message = "Hello";
  console.log(message); // OK
}
console.log(message); // Error: 'message' is not defined
```

You cannot declare another variable with the same name in the same scope if you've already declared it with "const".

No redeclaration

```
const value = 42;
const value = 100; // Error: Identifier 'value' has already
been declared
```

When using "const" with objects and arrays, the reference to the object or array itself is immutable, but the properties or elements within the object or array can still be modified.

Modifying object's properties and array's elements

```
const person = { name: "Alice", age: 30 };
person.age = 31; // Valid, modifies a property inside
the object
const numbers = [1, 2, 3];
numbers.push(4); // Valid, adds an element to the array
```

In summary, the "const" keyword is used to declare variables that are meant to remain constant after their initial assignment. It ensures immutability of the variable reference, but the properties or elements within objects and arrays declared with "const" can still be modified. Use "const" for values that should not be changed throughout the scope of the variable.

Manipulating Objects in JavaScript

In JavaScript, structuring and destructuring objects are techniques that allow for efficient data manipulation.

Step 1: Structuring an Object

Structuring an object involves defining a data structure for that object. You can create an object with a list of properties and their corresponding values. For example, you can create a person object with properties like name, age, and city as follows:

Creating the person object

```
const person = {
  name: "Gaby",
  age: 40,
  city: "Austin"
};
```

This allows us to access the values person.name (which is "Gaby"), person.age (which is 40), and person.city (which is "Austin").

Step 2: Object Destructuring

Object destructuring, on the other hand, allows you to extract object properties and use them independently. For instance, you can extract the name and age properties from the person object as follows:

Destructuring the person object

```
const { name, age } = person;
```

In this example, we create two variables, name and age, that correspond to properties of the same names in the person object. We can now use these variables independently of the rest of the object. Destructuring can also be used to pass arguments to a function in a more concise way. For example, you can create a function that takes an object person as an argument and displays the person's name and age:

Using destructuring in function definition

```
function displayNameAge({ name, age }) {
  console.log(`The name is ${name} and the age is ${age}`);
}
```

In this example, we use destructuring to extract the properties name and age from the person object that is passed as an argument. We can now call this function with the person object as follows:

Using the function

```
displayNameAge(person);
```

This will display "The name is Gaby and the age is 40" in the console.

In summary, object structuring and destructuring in JavaScript are powerful techniques that allow for efficient and concise data manipulation.

Step 3: Passing Objects as Function Parameters

In JavaScript, the notation { key1, key2 } is used in function parameters to perform object destructuring. This notation allows you to destructure a literal object by extracting the values associated with the specified properties and assigning them to variables with the same names as the properties.

Here's an example to illustrate its usage:

Object as a function parameter

```javascript
function displayDetails({ name, age }) {
  console.log(`Name: ${name}`);
  console.log(`Age: ${age}`);
}

const person = {
  name: "Gaby",
  age: 40,
  city: "Austin",
  profession: "Developer",
};
displayDetails(person);    // Displays "Name: Gaby" and
                           // "Age: 40"
```

In this example, the displayDetails() function takes an object as a parameter and destructures the object to extract values associated with the name and age properties. The extracted values are then used to display the person's details.

It's important to note that if a specified property in the destructuring notation does not exist in the object, its value will be undefined. Additionally, it's possible to rename the extracted variables using the syntax { property: newVariable }.

In summary, the { key1, key2 } notation in function parameters allows for object destructuring, extracting values associated with specified properties. This leads to more concise and readable code, avoiding direct property access within the function body.

Step 4: Using the "..." Notation with Objects

Let's now explain the "..." (three consecutive dots) notation with objects. The "..." notation in JavaScript, also known as the spread or rest operator, is used to spread or gather the elements of an array or an object.

When used with an object, the "..." notation creates a shallow copy of the original object, including all its properties and their values. For example:

Using the "..." notation with objects

```
const object1 = { x: 1, y: 2 };
const object2 = { ...object1 };
console.log(object2);     // { x: 1, y: 2 }
```

In this example, the "..." notation is used to spread the properties of object1 into object2. This creates a shallow copy of object1, with the same properties and values.

If you write const object2 = object1;, it does not do the same thing at all! This statement creates a variable object2 that has the same memory reference as object1, thus referencing the same content as object1. If you modify the content of object1 or object2, the other object will be modified in the same way.

The "..." notation can also be used to merge multiple objects into one. For example:

Merging objects with "..."

```
const object1 = { x: 1, y: 2 };
const object2 = { z: 3 };
const object3 = { ...object1, ...object2 };
console.log(object3);    // { x: 1, y: 2, z: 3 }
```

In this example, the "..." notation is used to merge the properties of objects object1 and object2 into a new object object3.

It's important to note that the "..." notation creates only a shallow copy of the original object. If the object contains properties that are themselves objects or arrays, these properties are not deeply copied and are still shared between the original object and the copy (since it's the references to objects or arrays that are copied, thus shared between the original object and the new object).

Manipulating Arrays in JavaScript

In JavaScript, an array is a data structure that allows you to store and access multiple elements as an ordered list.

Step 1: Structuring an Array

Structuring arrays in JavaScript refers to creating, initializing, and manipulating arrays to store and organize data.

Creating an array in JavaScript can be done in several ways. The most common way is to declare an empty array and add elements using the push() method. For example:

Creating an array using the push() method

```
let array = [];
array.push(1);
array.push(2);
array.push(3);
console.log(array);    // [1, 2, 3]
```

Another common method to create an array is by using the array literal notation, which allows you to declare and initialize an array in a single step. For example:

Creating an array using []

```
let array = [1, 2, 3];
console.log(array);    // [1, 2, 3]
```

Step 2: Array Destructuring

Array destructuring in JavaScript refers to extracting elements from an array into separate variables. This feature is useful for manipulating arrays in a more concise and readable manner. For example:

Array destructuring into separate variables

```
let array = [1, 2, 3];
let [firstElement, secondElement, thirdElement] = array;
console.log(firstElement);   // 1
console.log(secondElement);  // 2
console.log(thirdElement);   // 3
```

Step 3: Using the "..." Notation with Arrays

Destructuring also allows you to retrieve a portion of an array using the "..." syntax. For example:

Destructuring an array using the "..." notation

```
let array = [1, 2, 3, 4, 5];
let [a, b, ...rest] = array;
console.log(a);     // 1
console.log(b);     // 2
console.log(rest);  // [3, 4, 5]
```

In this example, the "..." notation is used to retrieve the remaining elements of the array after assigning the first two elements to the variables "a" and "b". The variable "rest" will contain the elements 3, 4, and 5 as an array, that is, [3, 4, 5].

Using Import and Export of Modules in JavaScript

In JavaScript, modules are code files that can contain functions, variables, and classes, which can be imported and used in other code files. Modules allow for structuring and organizing JavaScript code, making it more modular and easier to maintain.

There are several ways to define and import modules in JavaScript, but the most common method is using the import and export syntax. Modules can be exported using the export and export default keywords, and they can be imported using the import keyword.

Here's a simple example to illustrate the creation and usage of modules in JavaScript (file myModule.js):

File: myModule.js

```
export const myVariable = "Hello world";

export function myFunction() {
  console.log("This is my function");
}

export default class MyClass {
  constructor() {
    console.log("This is my class");
  }
}
```

We export the variable myVariable, the function myFunction(), and the JavaScript class MyClass in the module myModule.js.

In another JavaScript file (e.g., test.js), we import these previously exported elements:

File: test.js

```
import { myVariable, myFunction } from './myModule.js';
import MyClass from './myModule.js';

console.log(myVariable);
myFunction();
const myInstance = new MyClass();
```

You can also write the "import" statement on a single line as follows:

File: test.js

```
import MyClass, { myVariable, myFunction } from
'./myModule.js';

console.log(myVariable);
myFunction();
const myInstance = new MyClass();
```

This way, we have access to the exported elements from the myModule.js file in the test.js file.

Step 1: Using Modules in HTML Files

To use JavaScript modules in an HTML file, we use the <script> tag with the "type" attribute set to "module".

Here's an example of HTML code that imports a module named myModule.js:

File: index.html

```
<!DOCTYPE html>
<html>
<head>
  <title>Example of Using Modules in HTML</title>
</head>
<body>

  <h1>Example of Using Modules in HTML</h1>
```

```
<script type="module">
  import { myFunction } from './myModule.js';
  myFunction();
</script>
</body>
</html>
```

The message "This is my function" is displayed in the browser console, demonstrating that the myFunction() is successfully accessible in the JavaScript code of the HTML file.

Step 2: Using the "import" Statement

The "import" statement is used in JavaScript to import modules from one JavaScript file to another. The basic syntax for importing a module is as follows:

Importing data from a module

```
import { variableName, functionName } from './path/to/module';
```

This syntax allows you to import specific variables or functions from a module. The path to the module should be relative to the current JavaScript file.

Here are some examples of using the "import" statement in JavaScript:

Using "import" in a module

```
// Importing a specific variable
import { myVariable } from './myModule.js';

console.log(myVariable);
```

```
// Importing multiple variables and a function
import { myVar1, myVar2, myFunction } from './myModule.js';

console.log(myVar1);
console.log(myVar2);
myFunction();

// Importing all exported variables and functions
import * as myModule from './myModule.js';

console.log(myModule.myVar1);
console.log(myModule.myVar2);
myModule.myFunction();
```

In these examples, the "import" statement is used to import specific variables and functions from a module. In the last example, all exported variables and functions are imported using the * operator, and an alias myModule is created to access the exported elements.

It's important to note that the "import" statement can only be used in a module context. A JavaScript file must be explicitly marked as a module by using the "type=module" directive in the <script> tag of the calling HTML file.

Step 3: Using the "export" Statement

The "export" statement in JavaScript is used to export variables, functions, classes, or other elements from one JavaScript file to another. The exported elements can be used in other files by importing the module that contains them.

There are two main ways to export elements in JavaScript: using the "export" syntax or "export default" syntax.

The "export" syntax is used to export named elements. For example, to export a named variable myVariable and a named function myFunction from a file myModule.js, you can use the following syntax:

Exporting variables (file myModule.js)

```
export const myVariable = "Hello world";

export function myFunction() {
  console.log("This is my function");
}
```

The exported elements can then be imported into another file using the "import" statement. Here's an example:

Importing variables in another module

```
import { myVariable, myFunction } from './myModule.js';

console.log(myVariable); // Displays "Hello world"
myFunction(); // Displays "This is my function"
```

Step 4: Using the "export default" Statement

The "export default" syntax is used to export a default element from a module. For example, to export a default class from a file myModule.js, you can use the following syntax:

Using export default (file myModule.js)

```
export default class MyClass {
  constructor() {
    console.log("This is my class");
  }
}
```

In this example, the MyClass class is exported as the default. It can be imported into another file using the following syntax:

Importing variables in another module

```
import MyClass from './myModule.js';

const myInstance = new MyClass(); // Creates a new instance of
the MyClass class
```

In summary, the export statement in JavaScript allows you to export elements from a module to make them available in other JavaScript files. It can be used to export variables, functions, classes, or other elements and can be combined with the import statement to create modular and reusable JavaScript applications.

Step 5: Difference Between "export" and "export default" Statements

The decision to use "export" or "export default" in JavaScript depends on how you want to expose module elements and import them later.

The export syntax is used to export multiple named elements from a module. This means that when a module is imported, the exported elements must be imported with their original names and enclosed in curly braces.

For example:

Using export, then import

```
// In the file "myModule.js"
export const myVar1 = "Hello";
export const myVar2 = "World";
export function myFunction() {
```

```
  console.log("This is my function");
}

// In the file that imports the module
import { myVar1, myVar2, myFunction } from './myModule.js';
// with curly braces
```

In this example, the exported elements must be imported using their
original names and enclosed in curly braces. If we try to import an element
with a different name than the one specified in the export, an error will be
generated.

The export default syntax is used to export a default element from a
module. This means that the element exported as default can be imported
later using a name of our choice. Only one element can be exported as
default in a module, to avoid confusion.

JavaScript will understand that we want to import the default exported
element in a module because we import it without using the curly braces
notation, unlike elements exported using the "export" statement, which
are imported with the curly braces notation.

For example:

Using export default, then import

```
// In the file "myModule.js"
export default class MyClass {
  constructor() {
    console.log("This is my class");
  }
}

// In the file that imports the module
import MyCustomName from './myModule.js';   // without using
                                            curly braces

const myInstance = new MyCustomName();
```

In this example, the default exported element (the MyClass class) can be imported using a name of our choice (MyCustomName in this case). This can be useful if we want to give a more meaningful name to the imported element or avoid naming conflicts.

In summary, "export" is used to export multiple named elements from a module, while "export default" is used to export an element that will be considered the default one during import. The decision to use one or the other depends on how we want to expose module elements and how we want to import them into other files.

Using Arrow Functions in JavaScript

Arrow functions are a new function syntax introduced in ECMAScript 6 (ES6) to write functions in a more concise and readable way. Here are the main differences between arrow functions and traditional functions:

- More concise syntax: Arrow functions have a more concise syntax than traditional functions. Instead of the classic function() {function body}, arrow functions are written like this: () => {function body}.

- No bound "this" keyword: In traditional functions, the "this" keyword is bound to the object that calls the function. In arrow functions, "this" is bound to the lexical context in which the function is defined. This means that "this" in an arrow function refers to "this" in the parent scope (the value of "this" in an arrow function will be the same as that of the parent).

Apart from the concise writing aspect of arrow functions, the deciding factor to use them in JavaScript code is mostly the desired value for the "this" variable.

Let's now look at the syntax of these functions and then explain the value of "this" in each use case.

Step 1: Using Arrow Function Syntax

Let's start by examining the writing syntax of these functions. Here's an example:

Using traditional functions and arrow functions

```
// Traditional function to calculate the square of a number
function square(x) {
  return x * x;
}
```

```
// Arrow function to calculate the square of a number
const square2 = (x) => x * x;
```

```
// Using the function
console.log(square2(5)); // Result: 25
```

In this example, the first function is a traditional function that calculates the square of a number. The second function is the arrow version of the same function, which uses a more concise syntax. Both functions have the same functionality, but the arrow version is more concise and easier to read.

Note that the arrow function syntax includes parentheses around the parameters (in this case, x), followed by the arrow =>, and then the function body (in this case, x * x). The arrow version doesn't require the return keyword here because it automatically returns the calculated value.

Here's an example of an arrow function in JavaScript that uses the return statement:

Functions using the return keyword

```javascript
// Traditional function to find the largest number in an array
function findLargest(array) {
  let largest = 0;
  for (let i = 0; i < array.length; i++) {
    if (array[i] > largest) {
      largest = array[i];
    }
  }
  return largest;
}

// Arrow function to find the largest number in an array
const findLargest2 = (array) => {
  let largest = 0;
  for (let i = 0; i < array.length; i++) {
    if (array[i] > largest) {
      largest = array[i];
    }
  }
  return largest;
}

// Using the function
console.log(findLargest2([4, 8, 2, 10, 5])); // Result: 10
```

In this example, the first function is a traditional function that finds the largest number in an array. The second function is the arrow version of the same function, which uses a more concise syntax. Both functions have the same functionality, and the arrow version also uses the return statement to return the calculated value.

Note that the arrow function syntax still includes parentheses around the parameters and the => arrow, but this time there are also curly braces to delimit the function body. The return statement is used to return the calculated value.

Step 2: Understanding the Value of "this" in Arrow Functions

The value of "this" in an arrow function is determined by the lexical context in which the function is defined, unlike traditional functions where "this" is determined by how the function is called.

In an arrow function, "this" refers to the value of "this" in the parent scope. This means that if the arrow function is defined within an object, for example, "this" in the arrow function refers to the parent object, not the object that calls the function.

Here's an example to illustrate this concept:

Values of "this" in traditional functions and arrow functions

```
const obj = {
  name: "John",
  sayHello: function() {
    console.log(`Hello, my name is ${this.name}`);
    // "John" (this refers to obj)
  },
  sayHelloArrow: () => {
    console.log(`Hello, my name is ${this.name}`);
    // undefined (this refers to the parent of obj)
  }
}

obj.sayHello();       // Result: "Hello, my name is John"
obj.sayHelloArrow();  // Result: "Hello, my name is undefined"
```

In this example, the object "obj" contains two functions: sayHello()
and sayHelloArrow(). sayHello() is a regular function that uses "this" to
access the "name" property of the object, while sayHelloArrow() is an
arrow function that also uses "this" to access the "name" property

When the sayHello() function is called, "this" refers to the "obj" object,
allowing access to the "name" property and displaying it in the console.
However, when the sayHelloArrow() function is called, "this" refers to
the lexical context in which the function was defined, which is the global
context in this case. Therefore, this.name is undefined in the arrow
function, and undefined is displayed in the console.

Depending on the value of "this" that we want to access, we will use
either a regular function or an arrow function.

Using the map( ) and filter( ) Methods of the JavaScript Array Class

The map(callback) and filter(callback) methods are two commonly used
high-level functions in JavaScript for manipulating arrays (or collections
of objects). They are often used with React. Here's an explanation of
each method.

Step 1: Using the map( ) Method

The map(callback) method creates a new array by applying a given
function, here named callback(), to each element of the original array. The
map() method takes a callback() function as a parameter.

The callback() function is then applied to each element of the original array. This function can take up to three arguments:

- element: The current element being processed

- index (optional): The index of the current element being processed in the array

- array (optional): The original array on which we are applying the function

The map() method then returns a new array with the results of applying the callback() function to each original element. The resulting array will have the same length as the original array.

Here's a simple example for better understanding:

Using the map() method

```
const array = [1, 2, 3, 4, 5];

const doubledArray = array.map(function(element) {
  return element * 2;
});

console.log(doubledArray); // [2, 4, 6, 8, 10]
```

Here, we created an array with numbers, and then we used the map() method to create a new array with the same numbers, but multiplied by 2.

The map() method returns a new array constructed from the elements of the original array. The resulting array will have the same number of elements as the original array.

To reduce the number of elements in the resulting array, we will use the filter() method, which allows us to select the elements to be included in the resulting array (but without modifying them). Let's now look at the filter() method.

Step 2: Using the filter( ) Method

The filter(callback) method also creates a new array, but it filters the elements of the original array that satisfy a specified condition. This method also takes a callback() function as an argument, which will be applied to each element of the original array. This callback() function must return a boolean value: true if the element should be retained in the resulting array returned by the filter() method, false otherwise.

The callback() filter function also takes up to three arguments:

- element: The current element being processed

- index (optional): The index of the current element being processed in the array

- array (optional): The original array on which the function is being applied

The filter() method then returns a new array with all the elements of the original array that satisfy the specified condition.

Here's a simple example to better understand:

Using the filter() method

```
const array = [1, 2, 3, 4, 5];

const filteredArray = array.filter(function(element) {
  return element % 2 === 0;  // Returns true if the element is
even (element is kept), otherwise false
});

console.log(filteredArray); // [2, 4]
```

Here, we've created an array with numbers, and then we used the filter() method to create a new array with only the even numbers.

Step 3: Using the map( ) and filter( ) Methods in React

The map() and filter() methods are widely used in React to manipulate data arrays and generate user interface elements.

Here are some reasons why these methods are useful in React:

- List rendering:

  When you have a list of data in your React application, you can use the map() method to dynamically generate a list of user interface elements. For example, if you have a list of names that you want to display on the screen, you can use map() to generate a list item for each name in the list.

- Data filtering:

  The filter() method is useful for filtering a list of data based on certain conditions. For instance, you can filter a list of products to display only the products that are in stock or have a certain price.

- Data manipulation:

  By using the map() method, you can also manipulate the data in a list to create new data that can be used to generate user interface elements. For example, you can take a list of raw data and use map() to create a new list with elements transformed based on certain business rules.

- Performance:

  Using map() and filter() in React is often preferred
  over traditional "for" loops as it can improve
  performance. Indeed, the map() and filter()
  methods are optimized for array processing and can
  often be executed more efficiently than "for" loops.

In summary, the map() and filter() methods are useful in React for
dynamically generating user interface elements from data lists, filtering
data based on certain conditions, manipulating data to create new data,
and improving performance.

Using Promise Objects in JavaScript

Promise objects in JavaScript are used for handling asynchronous tasks,
which are tasks that don't complete immediately. A Promise object
represents a value that may not be available immediately but will be
resolved (i.e., become available) at some point in the future.

Step 1: Promise Object Definition

Promise objects are often created as return values from functions
because they provide a clearer and more structured way of handling
asynchronous tasks.

When an asynchronous task is executed, it doesn't immediately return
a result, as it needs to perform an operation that may take time (such
as an HTTP request or file reading). While waiting for this operation to
complete, the code that follows continues to execute, potentially causing
synchronization and blocking issues.

Promise objects are used to address this issue. They provide a clear and structured way to handle asynchronous tasks by returning an object that represents the promise of a future result. This object can be used to attach callback functions that will be called once the asynchronous task is completed, and the result is available.

For example, a function that performs an HTTP request can return a Promise object representing the promise of the request's result. Callbacks can then be attached to this Promise object using the then() and catch() methods to handle successful results or errors that may occur during the execution of the asynchronous task.

In summary, the Promise object is created as a return value from a function to handle asynchronous tasks in a structured manner by returning an object representing the promise of a future result and attaching callbacks to handle results or errors.

A Promise object can be in one of the following three states:

- "pending": The initial state of the Promise object, indicating that the asynchronous task is currently being executed

- "resolved": The state in which the Promise object is resolved with a value

- "rejected": The state in which the Promise object is rejected with an error reason

The Promise object exposes two methods for handling the results of the asynchronous task:

- The then() method: Used to handle the result if the task is successfully resolved

- The catch() method: Used to handle errors that occur if the task is rejected

By using Promise objects, it's possible to perform asynchronous tasks in JavaScript more efficiently and in a way that's easier to read and maintain.

To understand the use of Promise objects, let's take an example where we don't use them and then the same example where we do.

Step 2: Without Using Promise Objects

Here's an example without using Promise objects:

Let's say we want to load images from a server and display them in our application. Without Promise objects, we would have to use callbacks to handle the asynchrony:

Without using Promise objects

```javascript
function loadImage(url, callback) {
  const img = new Image();
  img.onload = function() {
    // no error
    callback(null, img);
  };
  img.onerror = function() {
    // error
    callback("Unable to load the image.", null);
  };
  img.src = url;  // image loading
}

loadImage("https://example.com/image.jpg",
function(error, img) {
  if (error) {
    console.error(error);
```

```
  } else {
    document.body.appendChild(img);
  }
});
```

This example uses the Image object to load an image from the server. The loadImage() function takes the image URL and a callback function as arguments. This callback will be invoked once the image has been loaded. After the image is loaded, further processing can take place within the callback function, allowing for handling of the asynchrony. The callback function has two arguments: a possible error and the loaded img (image) itself.

Step 3: Using Promise Objects

Now, here's the same example using Promise objects:

Using Promise objects

```
function loadImage(url) {
  return new Promise(function(resolve, reject) {
    const img = new Image();
    img.onload = function() {
      // no error
      resolve(img);
    };
    img.onerror = function() {
      // error
      reject("Unable to load the image.");
    };
    img.src = url;  // image loading
  });
}
```

```
loadImage("https://example.com/image.jpg")
  .then(function(img) {
    document.body.appendChild(img);
  })
  .catch(function(error) {
    console.error(error);
  });
```

Here, the loadImage() function returns a Promise object that is resolved with the image if the image loading succeeds, or is rejected with an error message if it fails. By using the then() method, we can handle the image once it has been loaded, and with the catch() method, we can handle errors that occur.

The use of Promise objects in this example makes the code more readable and easier to understand and provides simplified error handling.

Using "async" and "await" Statements in JavaScript

The "async" and "await" statements are features of JavaScript that make working with Promise objects even more readable and understandable for handling asynchronous tasks.

By using "async" and "await" statements, code can be written synchronously (i.e., with sequentially following instructions) while still effectively managing asynchronous tasks. The "async" statement is used to mark a function as asynchronous, allowing the use of the "await" statement within that function.

The "await" statement is used to wait for the resolution of a Promise object before continuing the code execution. This avoids the use of callbacks and results in code that is easier to read and understand.

For example, here's a usage example of Promise objects to make an HTTP request. We will then see how to write the same code using "async" and "await" statements.

Using Promise objects to make an HTTP request

```
fetch("https://api.example.com/data")
  .then(response => response.json())
  .then(data => console.log(data))
  .catch(error => console.error(error));
```

The fetch() and json() methods in JavaScript each return a Promise object, enabling the use of the then() and catch() methods on these methods.

Now, here's how we can rewrite this code using "async" and "await" statements:

Using "async" and "await" statements to make an HTTP request

```
async function getData() {
  try {
    const response = await fetch("https://api.example.
    com/data");
    const data = await response.json();
    console.log(data);
  } catch (error) {
    console.error(error);
  }
}

getData();
```

Here, the getData() function is marked as "async", which allows (within the getData() function) the use of the "await" statement to wait for the resolution of Promise objects returned by the fetch() function and the json() method. The use of "async" and "await" statements enables writing code that is more readable and easier to understand while efficiently managing asynchronous tasks.

In summary, the use of "async" and "await" statements provides an easier and more readable way to utilize Promise objects for handling asynchronous tasks. This helps avoid the use of callbacks and reduces code complexity.

Creating an Asynchronous Function That Utilizes JavaScript's "await" Statement

Let's now see how to create an asynchronous function that can use the "await" statement. For this purpose, the function using "await" should fall into one of the following two cases:

- The function returns a Promise object. This is the case, for example, with the previous fetch() and json() methods.

- The function is declared with the "async" keyword. In this case, the function's return is always considered as a Promise object (even if the function returns another value).

Let's examine these two cases now.

Step 1: Using "await" with a Function That Returns a Promise Object

For "await" to be used with a function, the function can return a Promise object or be declared with the "async" keyword.

Here's an example of a function that returns a Promise object:

Function returning a Promise object

```
function wait(ms) {
  return new Promise(resolve => setTimeout(resolve, ms));
}
```

The wait(ms) function takes a number of milliseconds as input and returns a Promise object that will resolve after the specified number of milliseconds. The function utilizes the setTimeout() function to trigger the resolution of the Promise object after a specified delay.

To use the wait(ms) function with the "await" statement, you simply need to call it within a function marked with "async", like this:

Usage of "await" in an "async" function

```
async function myFunction() {
  console.log("Start");    // Display "Start"
  await wait(2000);        // Wait for 2 seconds
  console.log("End");      // Then display "End" (after 2
seconds)
}

myFunction();
```

This myFunction() function uses the "await" statement to wait for the resolution of the Promise object returned by the wait() function. The function prints "Start" to the console, waits for two seconds using "await wait(2000)", and then prints "End" to the console.

In cases where the wait(ms) function wants to return a value, you can simply provide that value ("value") as a parameter in the resolve(value) function call.

The wait(ms) function becomes as follows:

Function wait(ms) that returns a value

```
function wait(ms) {
  return new Promise(resolve => setTimeout(() =>
rcsolve("Waiting for " + ms + " ms"), ms));
}
```

We can no longer simply indicate setTimeout(resolve, ms) as before, because now we need to explicitly call the resolve() function and pass the return value as a parameter. Hence, the new syntax is written as setTimeout(() => resolve(value), ms).

We use the value returned by the wait(ms) function as follows:

Using the value returned by the wait(ms) function

```
async function myFunction() {
  console.log("Start");            // Display "Start"
  const result = await wait(2000); // Wait for 2 seconds
  console.log(result);             // Display the result
                                   // returned by the wait()
                                   // function
  console.log("End");              // Then display "End"
}

myFunction();
```

Step 2: Using "await" with a Function Declared with "async"

This is the second way to use the "await" statement when calling a function. The function must have been declared using the "async" keyword during its definition.

A function declared with the "async" keyword is considered to return a Promise object. Therefore, it can be used when called with the then() and catch() methods or used with the "await" keyword.

Using the myFunction() function with "await"

```javascript
function wait(ms) {
  return new Promise(resolve => setTimeout(() =>
resolve("Waiting for " + ms + " ms"), ms));
}
async function myFunction() {
  console.log("Start");             // Display "Start"
  const result = await wait(2000);  // Wait for 2 seconds
  console.log(result);              // Display the result
                                    // returned by the wait()
                                    // function
  console.log("End");               // Then display "End"
  return "myFunction(): Waiting for 2000ms";
}

async function myMainFunction() {
  const result = await myFunction();
  console.log("result =", result);
}

myMainFunction();
```

Since the myFunction() is declared with "async", it can be used within a new function called myMainFunction() using the "await" keyword. The result returned by myFunction() will be used as the return value in myMainFunction(), asynchronously (after waiting for two seconds).

The same process can be written using promises and the then() / catch() methods:

Using promises instead of await

```
function wait(ms) {
  console.log("wait(" + ms + ")");
  return new Promise(resolve => setTimeout(() =>
resolve("Waiting for " + ms + " ms"), ms));
}

async function myFunction() {
  console.log("Start");             // Display "Start"
  const result = await wait(2000);  // Wait for 2 seconds
  console.log(result);              // Display the result
                                    // returned by the wait()
                                    // function
  console.log("End");               // Then display "End"
  return "myFunction(): Waiting for 2000ms";
}

myFunction().then((res) => { console.log(res) });
```

The then(res) method used on the promise myFunction() allows retrieving the result of the promise, which is the string "myFunction() : Waiting for 2000ms", in the parameter res.

Conclusion of the Book

Master React in 5 Days is a comprehensive guide that enables the reader to learn the fundamentals of the JavaScript library React in just five days. The book covered key concepts of component creation, JSX usage, event handling, hooks utilization, and much more.

The reader has gained a strong understanding of React and can now use it to build modern web applications. The skills acquired from the book enable the reader to work on real projects and create interactive user interfaces, forms and controls, dashboards, ecommerce applications, and much more.

Furthermore, the reader can use the skills acquired from the book to continue learning and exploring React. Online resources are plentiful, and there are numerous complementary tools and libraries that can be utilized to enhance React skills.

In summary, *Master React in 5 Days* has been an enriching educational experience for you, I hope! The book has provided a solid understanding of the React library and has enabled the reader to develop practical web development skills. The skills gained from the book serve as a strong foundation for becoming a competent and efficient React developer and for continuing to explore the many possibilities that React offers in the future.

Index

A, B

App() function, 20
Autostart, 88–91

C

callback() function, 264, 265
catch() methods, 187, 268, 272
change() function, 94
clearInterval() function, 28, 37
"const" keyword, 243
Counter() function, 35, 46
createContext() method, 130, 131
create-react-app command, 9, 16
Custom hook
    component update, 173–178
    data formatting, 190–193
    fetch data from server, 184, 186,
        187, 189, 190
    filters displayed data,
        193, 195–197
    limits counter value, 168–172
    reactive variable, 178–183

D

DevTools utility, 25
displayDetails() function, 248

Document object model (DOM), 4, 6, 7

E

Ecommerce applications, 240
Event handling
    click events, button
        capturing an event, 78, 79
        component, 78
        counter component, 88–92
        increment button, 79–82
        periodic counter, start
          button, 83–87
    elements, 77
    input field
        App component, 93, 94
        digits, 95, 97
        displayed counter, 104–107
        display value, 95
        focus() method, 97, 99
        real-time sum, 100–103

F

fetch() and json() methods, 272
fetch(url) method, 184, 187
filter() method, 69, 195, 216, 265

Printed in the United States
by Baker & Taylor Publisher Services